ASPEN/DREAMS & DILEMMAS
love letter to a small town

ASPEN/DREAMS & DILEMMAS
love letter to a small town

Peggy Clifford and John M. Smith

THE SWALLOW PRESS INC.

CHICAGO

First Edition
Copyright © 1970 by Peggy Clifford and John M. Smith
All rights reserved
Printed in the United States of America

Published by
The Swallow Press Incorporated
1139 South Wabash Avenue
Chicago, Illinois 60605

LIBRARY OF CONGRESS CATALOG CARD NUMBER 79-81962

To Freddie Fisher
whose courage, honesty, and humor
meant so much to Aspen and to us
and whose memory burns so bright
PC and JMS

Wavering between the profit and the loss
In this brief transit where the dreams cross
The dreamcrossed twilight between birth and dying
                                T. S. Eliot, *Ash Wednesday*

Contents

1 The Problem 1

2 The Place 13

3 The People 71

4 The Process 143

5 The Prospect 195

6 A Postscript 211

Appendix 215
Photographers, Photo Captions,
Acknowledgments

Chapter 1 / The Problem

The American small town, like the bald eagle, is vanishing from our landscape and our minds.

In another generation, there may be young people who not only have never seen a small town but don't even know what one is. Magazines devote endless pages to the problems, the future, and the character of big cities, but scant attention is paid to the plight or the pleasures of the small towns. They have become passé, out-dated, like grandfather's flivver or grandmother's butter churn. As depicted on television, small towns are havens for bumpkins, morons, homely philosophers, and brutes; down-at-the-heels amalgams of picket fences, rose bushes, sleepy streets, false-front stores, and corn at least as high as an elephant's eye. Small towns don't make headlines unless they are demolished by tornadoes, inhabited by mass murderers or astronauts, or over-run with locusts. Yet the pressures that are making our cities increasingly intolerable are reaching out into rural America, too. Because no small town measures up to today's volatile demands, all small towns are in jeopardy in our affluent society.

Some small towns—primarily in the South and the Midwest—are simply withering away, dying in the noonday sun. They are too far away from the action. Their young have abandoned them. Big corporations have squeezed little farmers out of a livelihood, off the land and into the cities, where they wander desolate and unskilled, working at menial jobs or relying on welfare. Many businesses in rural America have closed up forever, and much of the prime space on Main Street, U.S.A. is now empty, furnished solely with cobwebs and remnants of old, soured dreams. America's dying small towns are, literally and figuratively, going nowhere but down and out.

Other small towns are being absorbed by large urban centers. This is a less painful and slower kind of dying, but dying is dying; it always ends badly. Failure of character is, after all, as ultimately disastrous as failure of heart. In the absorption process, these small towns lose their identity and their independence. They become suburbs. The very name is demeaning.

Sooner or later, the small-town-turned-suburb combines the worst aspects of the small town with the worst aspects of the big city. Like some small towns, the suburb is often provincial, narrow in view, and mean in spirit. Like most big cities, it is usually anonymous, fragmented, and overbuilt.

It is no wonder that novelists and satirists have pictured the suburbs as mammoth barbecue pits where martini-drinking, fun-loving, wife-swapping neurotics frolic under the light of specially imported, authentic reproduction gas lamps.

These soulless suburbs gradually begin to look alike and feel alike—whether they're in Illinois, New York,

or California. If something's *in* in Lake Forest, it's *in* in New Rochelle and Burlingame, too. That splendid space of trees and meadows and miles of empty highway that used to isolate and insulate all small towns, that made them serenely exciting oases of cottonwood trees and clapboard houses in an empty, rolling wilderness has been filled with shopping centers, discount houses, gaudy drive-ins, gas stations, and the other garish trappings of affluence. In suburbia, everything runs into everything else and the urban cancers—crime, congestion, unrest, pollution—are gradually eroding suburban streets and souls. Megalopolis is force-feeding its blights into its satellites.

Finally, some small towns change or compromise to survive. In the Colorado Rockies, Aspen, Crested Butte, and Breckenridge have returned from oblivion to eminence as ski and summer resorts. Once mining and ranching towns, they now rely on tourists for sustenance. In New Hampshire and Vermont, Wolfeboro and Stowe have switched their focus from the farmer to the vacationer. The Vermont Development Corporation recently ran an ad plumping tourism. Under the headline, "There's a country road I'm going to take someday," it featured a photo of a lovely, pastoral, tree-lined lane and a coupon with which to send for the "Vermont Vacation Kit." If enough people send for the kit, that lovely lane will become a four-lane, sign-lined highway. In California, Carmel and Monterey, once proud and quirky places where artists and writers mingled with fishermen and canners and all benefited, have become quaint and cute tourist traps. Robinson Jeffers and John Steinbeck have been replaced in the area's pantheon of genius by plump, slick screenwriters, all of whom are going to write the Great American Novel when the cocktail parties stop. The decline from proud and quirky to quaint and cute is part of the process that turns

a town into a commodity. And, too often—with tourists and developers working in diabolic unison—successful resorts are more commodities than towns. The ease and economy of jet travel can turn any town anywhere—if it is beautiful or interesting or unique—into a colony of megalopolis, a playground for urbanites.

Some communities enter into the colonization process willingly. They prefer compromise to death. And so —like Vermont and many other tourist-oriented areas— they set about to sell themselves. Some sell serenity. Others sell clean, uncluttered beaches or snow and scenery. Still others market clean air and peace, all items that urbanites are willing to pay dearly for. The irony is that as the urbanites rush in, the serenity and peace vanish, the beaches and mountain slopes become crowded with people, the scenery vanishes behind cars, buses, billboards, and camper trucks and the clean air and water are fouled.

Other small towns are reluctant resorts. Their residents are happy with what they have: little cash, much cachet. But their abundance of natural resources becomes their downfall. They are discovered. Travel agencies begin touting their unusual merits to restless urbanites. People come back raving about the beauty, the peace, the quality of snow or surf. The airlines offer irresistible package plans. And the town that simply wanted to be left alone is suddenly on the map. The developers move in with bankrolls, big plans, and bulldozers, sincerely believing that they can improve on what nature has wrought and residents have left alone. The resort business is booming in America. Skiers alone spent over $1 billion last year.

This process of death, absorption, or transformation is accelerating all over the country. But some small town residents, while willing to admit the necessity of change, are unwilling to simply lie down and let the

monster progress run over them.

Thus, the confrontation between past and present, dream and reality, aesthetics and economics, pioneers and dudes is often angry and occasionally ugly. It is once again settlers protecting their hard-won land from marauders. In towns around the country, marauders are armed with heavy weapons and are looking for an opening. The marauders may have more strength, but the settlers are very determined. There is only one fundamental difference in this modern shootout: the ammunition is money and, to date, no one in America has ever been able to win against the overwhelming power of money.

Aspen, Colorado has lived in a state of seige for nearly a decade. One of the great small towns, one of the few to combine the sophistication and the freedom of the city with the beauty and serenity of the country, it will not die, it is too remote to be absorbed, but it is under fire and it is changing.

Chapter 2 / The Place

Some people maintain churlishly that Aspen, Colorado does not exist. They say it's a myth, a mood, an attitude, a condition . . . but not a real place.

In fact, Aspen is all of these things: ephemeral and real, wispy and solid, memory and fact, a mercurial town, hard to catch, harder to hold onto. It has been famous and prosperous twice—first on such substantial stuff as silver wrenched from the mountains by zealous and hard men; more lately on such amorphous stuff as snow and culture.

Today, as always, Aspen bewitches many, bewilders others, and actually irritates a few stern servants of reality who demand to know, "What's so special here?" Part past (known), part future (unknown), Aspen shimmers in the present, a frontier circa 1970, where the settlers battle the marauders for control and where people still have time to wonder about such unprofitable things as nature and art and life itself.

Aspen rambles and sprawls across the valley floor and creeps up the lower slopes of the mountains, which are an integral part of the townscape. Much more than mere scenery, they inspire, they refresh, they dominate the eye and the mind, and, periodically, they kill. 7,900 feet above sea level, Aspen has mountains on three sides. They loom large and eternal.

To the east a jumble of mountains steps up to the Continental Divide, which runs through a raw, barren meadow at the top of Independence Pass, only thirty miles from Aspen. Here, in some secret crevice, 4,000 feet above Aspen, the Roaring Fork begins and its waters, largely melting snow, tumble 1,200 miles to the Pacific.

To the north of Aspen is Red Mountain. Once a vast ranch, it is now creased with roads and studded with expensive modern houses which hang like baubles on the steep slope. The view from these houses sweeps over town and mountains, changes with the sun, and ends in a distant tangle of snowy peaks and sky.

Surrounded by an infinity of mountains, Aspen is ruled by one: Ajax, which rises dramatically from the south edge of downtown Aspen. There it is, you think. My God, there it is! Town and mountain live together in rough harmony. Aspen, after all, could not exist without the bounty of Ajax. In the 1880's, the mountain's silver made mine owners rich. In the 1970's, its snow makes the Aspen Skiing Corporation rich and Aspen's shopowners, restauranteurs, and lodgeowners at least prosperous. Ajax has the irrevocable strength and pride of natural things. The miners nicknamed it Silver Queen because they saw in her the profile of a stern and dignified lady wreathed in miles of varicolored lace which preserved her secrets and her grandeur. Ajax is a big and intricate mountain. Today, as many as 2,500 skiers (more than the year-round population of the town) go

to its slopes daily, ride up the chairlifts, and vanish into the miles of trails and acres of bowls which cannot be seen from the town. (The mountain that made Aspen famous twice is officially called Aspen now, but many residents persist in calling it Ajax, after an old mining claim.)

The town of Aspen looks nothing like other small towns. It is not lush and sweetly sinister like some Southern towns. It is not prosperous and comfortable like some Midwestern towns. It is not orderly and elegant like old New England towns. And, most surprisingly, it does not have that lean and hungry look, that dusty sparseness of Western towns.

There is a spaciousness about Aspen; yet at its widest point it is only seven blocks across. There is a looseness, an easiness; yet its grid is rigid and formal, all straight lines and right angles. There is a clarity; yet its buildings are totally mismatched. There is a generosity, a gentleness, a warmth; yet it is assaulted by snow from November through April. In appearance and posture, Aspen is simultaneously handsome and ugly, gracious and rude, like the face of a great character actor. It bears the marks of both its original settlers who brought bits and pieces of their birthplaces and planted them in Aspen and its latterday settlers who wanted, for the most part, to forget the places they left behind and to make something new and different— and perhaps better.

Aspen is a superb example of individuality and time at work. Visual ironies are in abundance. Heavy Victorian edifices, aging gracefully, lean in the wind. Chunks of cinderblock assembled without art are rude reminders of the increasing influence of efficiency and economy. Angular new buildings indicate graphically that each man has a different idea of beauty. Precise and plain clapboard houses stand primly in rows.

Chalets, authentic and imitation, try to ape the Alps. A few new and giant structures blank out large portions of sun and sky, leaving their neighbors in the shade. Victorian masterpieces, echoing that sturdy frivolity of the 1890's, turn up in unexpected places. Somehow it all holds together and pleases the eye. There is a weird coherence. No neon signs, nothing that blisters the eyeball, nothing which demands to be remembered . . . and yet you do remember.

It has a sort of frowsy elegance which sticks in the mind. The downtown area is relatively small: only four blocks square. It is a bizarre blend of Fifth Avenue and the frontier, Carnaby Street and cow country, Montmartre and the mountains, Greenwich Village and ghost town. In season, winter or summer, night or day, the streets are crowded and boisterous, full of tourists rushing about at their usual double-time city pace, determined to enjoy themselves at all costs; and residents, moving more slowly, dressed more casually, perpetually surprised at the commotion. Large plate-glass windows show the passerby a variety of scenes: red-faced people grinning as they destroy delicate French pastries with their All-American teeth; laughing people all atilt over beer and peanuts; sombre scholars browsing through books; ladies with sculptured hair musing over rare glass from Venice or peasant dresses from the Yucatan; prosperous gentlemen in expensive sweaters choosing an expensive scotch, while a ragged old man reaches automatically for a cheap wine; serious men sitting behind serious desks or drawing boards, striving, in the midst of this carnival, to keep the wheels turning. The action on the street is welded to the action in the shops, restaurants, and offices. The people on the inside and the people on the outside are all part of the same play. It is convivial and chaotic, like the last tumultuous scene in a Verdi opera when everyone is on stage at once. It is a perpetual

Saturday night in an old mining town.

After dark, Aspen explodes and people turn away from the mountains and chase after more earthbound rainbows. There is a Rabelaisian lustiness about it. People eating and drinking and laughing and dancing with uncommon fervor. Everyone seems to be celebrating something: new snow, a day in the sun, a superb concert, the arrival of friends, the departure of enemies, the phases of the moon, a fat trout finally hooked. These nocturnal rites wham into the early hours of morning, but by 2:30 the streets are empty, inhabited only by moonlight and shadows.

Downtown Aspen is a random mix of activities, enterprises, and architectural styles. One graceful building houses a Mexican restaurant, a book store, a drug store, a candle shop, and a lawyer's office. Another has apartments on the second floor; the first floor contains a utility office, a real estate firm, a gift shop, a photo shop, a dentist's office, and a French restaurant which would delight Victorian ghosts. Fragments of ancient advertisements embellish many of the buildings' dusty brick walls. These forerunners of billboards are dim and faded and the products they tout no longer exist. But they are visible proof of another era, messages from the past. Most of the big buildings in downtown Aspen are old buildings. Any one of them would fit comfortably in the lobby of a modern skyscraper, for they are really not very big at all. None of these old buildings is more than three stories high nor half-a-block long. But they are big enough to give the business district substance, style, and scale. More dense and reliable than beautiful, they, perhaps more than anything else, hold the townscape together, underscoring the strange symmetry that downtown Aspen has always had, in spite of its casual airs and peculiar juxtapositions. For all its impressive shops and four-star restaurants, for all its slightly askew

cosmopolitan flavor, the area is intimate, almost cozy. And it is very small. You could lose downtown Aspen in Times Square and never find it again.

In the off-season, spring or fall, downtown Aspen is sleepy, lazy, and nearly peaceful. Residents stroll aimlessly around the almost empty streets, pausing to talk to friends they lost in the season's maelstrom. A lot of tire-kicking and cloud-watching goes on. Many restaurants and stores simply close, leaving their windows grey and empty of action. Their owners retreat to Mexico or their own backyards. There is suddenly an abundance of parking spaces. After several weeks of off-season, it is difficult to remember the mid-season madness. This serenity, this quiet in Aspen in spring and fall would surprise a great many of the revelers who only see the town when it's on—exciting, colorful, and action-packed; but spring and fall respites are vital to residents who prefer Aspen the town to Aspen the commodity.

Like every small town, Aspen has a Main Street. Wide and straight, it bullets fifteen blocks from the west edge of town to a bend of the Roaring Fork. It is also part of state highway 82. With the gay and gallant Hotel Jerome, the handsome, modern library, some grand old Victorian houses restored to their fin-de-siecle fanciness, the ancient and solid Pitkin County Courthouse with its vast, airy offices, and St. Mary's Church, Main Street is an almost stately avenue.

Beyond the downtown area, on both sides of Main Street, in all seasons, the landscape is varied and serene. It is pastoral in places, occasionally shabby, sometimes stylish, but never monotonous. The streets are wide, unpaved in places, and from some points on some streets you can look from midtown Aspen to the jagged horizon twenty miles to the west. There are few sidewalks. Cyclists, pedestrians, cars, horses, buggies, dogs, and children share the streets. Edging the streets, irrigation

ditches left over from another era sometimes babble with water, cooling the air and keeping trees green.

In the west end of town, which fans out into the Roaring Fork Valley, elderly cottonwood trees line the streets and in late afternoon make long, slanty shadows in the air. In the east end, which reaches to the rock skirts of the mountains, dark comes earlier. The sun vanishes behind the rocky, hooked west ridge of Ajax at 2:30 in the afternoon in mid-winter and the black profile of the Silver Queen stretches out over the town.

Beyond the city limits, to east and west, are additional residential areas. To the east, the houses are lost and invisible in thick stands of aspen trees. To the west, they are spread out on a vast treeless meadow. A lovely pocket-sized cemetery gives a ghostly grace to the neighborhood. Beyond the houses is a golf course. Other Aspenites live up the Castle and Maroon Creek canyons, which curve south and southwest into the mountains from a common junction near the golf course. Further down the valley, northwest, are the towns of Woody Creek and Snowmass (not to be confused with Snowmass-at-Aspen), ranching communities with their own post office-stores, then Basalt, with 400 residents, then Carbondale, with about 900 residents, then, at the mouth of the valley, Glenwood Springs, with 4,000 residents, a big town by western Colorado standards. It is forty-two miles from Aspen to Glenwood Springs. There the Roaring Fork empties into the long, broad Colorado River. All of these towns share Aspen's natural assets, yet it is Aspen, the most remote of all, which has captured the hearts and imaginations of so many people; it is Aspen which is known all over the world; it is Aspen which exemplifies the dilemma of the American small town today.

There is no special or exalted neighborhood in Aspen, no special or exalted street. Some yards are neat

and well-manicured. Some look like mini-hayfields. Others light up summer's dusk with silent explosions of color. A few cynics have replaced their flower beds with gravel. Occasionally, one encounters a cow or several horses patiently putting up with city life. Some barns have been turned into smart House Beautiful studios. Others are still barns, though they more often house Jaguars and lawn mowers than cows and horses. These neighborhoods are very, very quiet. The silence is now and then punctuated by a high-hopeful child's voice announcing a triumph or summoning a dog to dinner . . . or an imperious owl hoot . . . or a dog signaling the arrival of a stranger or a high-powered car scudding over the weather-dented street. Most often, however, the silence is layered and profound. Aspen has a texture which is somehow mellow in a cold climate.

Because it is in the mountains, surrounded by a wilderness which can be pushed back but not diminished, because the weather has such an overbearing influence, because the sky is its nearest neighbor, Aspen—for all its fame and prominence—remains more connected to the natural world than to the man-made world. Everything in Aspen is affected by nature. The town's economy is based on snow. Heavy rain can disrupt a summer concert. Many houses have "mud rooms" in lieu of vestibules. A major portion of the municipal budget must be devoted to snow removal. Buildings must be constructed of extra-durable materials and padded with extra-effective insulation to withstand winter's onslaughts. Vegetable gardens are, because of the bittersweetly brief summers, chancy enterprises. Snow in May, which is not infrequent, can kill all the new flowers. After a cold seige, frozen and burst pipes are commonplace. Television, telephone, and electric cable systems are frequently knocked out by storms. Dogs sometimes die of poison put out for coyotes. And deer

sometimes come to nibble, along with skunks, in Aspen neighborhoods.

There is much drama in the seasons. Winter is black and white, crisp and cold, dangerous and beautiful. Spring is beige turning green, often muddy, always erratic and teasing. Summer is luxuriously green, warm and sweet-smelling days, cool blue nights, lazy and hectic all at once. Fall is brilliant orange and yellow, slashing shadows, long, hazy mists, strong true reflections and subtle blurs of grey.

Aspen residents do not want to tame the country or the weather; they simply want to know it, to become part of it. Sometimes they are killed by it. The young mother of four children is swept away in an avalanche. A writer slides off the road in a jeep and freezes to death before anyone finds him. There is no question that the mountain wilderness is dangerous and, occasionally, brutal, but its temptations are almost irresistible. Skiers go out in violent storms or below-zero air when there is new snow. Men climb mountains in midwinter. Hunters camp out in down bags on iced nights so they can begin their primitive quest at first light. People ride patched inner tubes through river rapids. Men still hike overland from Leadville to Aspen or ski across the mountains from Aspen to Crested Butte. Some families pack into the high country every weekend of the summer, spend the night, and pack out again. These overland trips range from twenty to a hundred miles through some of America's roughest and most primitive country. There is no practical reason for such a hike, but Aspen residents are not always practical about nature. Small boys still crack rocks open thoughtfully, looking for silver ore. Little girls still wonder, sitting in their warm houses on cold nights, where the deer go when deep snow obliterates their trails. This process of familiarization, kinship, and connection has been going

on since 1879, when Aspen was founded. Each generation must study the territory and know it anew.

Children lead Huckleberry Finn lives in Aspen. Their playground is right outside their doors and it is infinite. They begin to sense and appreciate the size of the country when they are very young. They dig caves in rusty mine tailings at the foot of Smuggler Mountain. They follow trails made by miners' boots in the 1880's to the Durant mine. They chase butterflies along the meandering path of the Roaring Fork, squishing through the bogs around Hallam Lake where Aspen's ladies iceskated eighty-five years ago and where now a wild game refuge has been made, just outside the city limits. They walk the route of the Denver and Rio Grande railroad which once hauled millions of dollars in silver ore out of the valley and now runs no more. They go fishing at the Slaughterhouse bridge at the base of Red Butte, one of the world's smallest, strangest, and most individualistic mountains which rises—like a daft pyramid—out of the valley. To look for fossils, they ride their bikes out to the Shale Bluffs, where the highway curves treacherously between steep, crumbling cliffs and a 500-foot drop to the river. Barefoot, barelegged, but very stylish in English hardhats, they ride high-life horses down Main Street.

And like their parents, they enjoy clowning. There seem to be more parades in Aspen than in most towns and they are wild and absurd affairs. Volunteer firemen appear, riding tiny scooters. Someone usually turns up, serious and solitary, carrying a float from a toilet. A walrus right out of *Alice in Wonderland,* signifying nothing, strolls along, playing a violin. Frazzled, hungover floats careen through the streets, bearing weird and abstract messages. A philosopher might categorize these parades as existential philandering, but they are more often simply vehicles for spending excess energy and

high spirits or escaping the lowdown, bad time blues. As author-anthropologist Theodora Krober, who grew up in a small Colorado mountain town, said of life there, "There are no neutral moments." A kind of mood lightning afflicts most Aspenites.

The contrast between the bustle and frenzy of Aspen and the absolute solitude and serenity of the forest and rivers is total. Complete silence and natural solace are only five minutes from the midtown commotion. In a quiet exodus, some Aspen residents have simply moved into the woods to live in houses they have designed and built out of native materials. These dwellings are often strangely elegant, despite their primitive equipage. They may not have bathrooms, but they usually have hi-fi systems and so it is possible to play Bach for an audience composed entirely of birds. Nature, as served up in the Roaring Fork Valley, is heady stuff. One becomes easily addicted to the uninterrupted sky, to the endless rolling out of mountains and valleys, meadows and streams, to the company of birds and beavers, deer and trout. Aspen is, after all, only a tiny circle of light and noise in a cool, green, still immensity and that cool, green stillness reaches into the clamorous circle and blunts its edge.

As one of only a handful of sports which is intimately involved with nature, skiing is an ideal vocation or avocation for many Aspenites. It parallels their feeling of how life should be—free, graceful, and unencumbered. There is a point of no return, a moment when a person becomes committed to skiing and its unique sensations. His values, the very order of his life, change. He becomes a more natural man, easier with himself and others. Some skiers wear infinity in their eyes. To understand Aspen, it is necessary to understand the strange lure of the mountains, the wilderness, and the snow.

Part clown, part sophisticate, Aspen is the brat of

the Rockies, sassy, unconventional, a big spender in pinch-pocket country, slightly askew, irreverent. Aspen plays Gatsby to Colorado's Babbitt.

II

As American towns go, Aspen had a late start. Until 1879, only mountain animals and a few Ute Indians had set foot in the high meadow which became Aspen. At the head of an unexplored valley, it might still be a beautiful, remote meadow, but for the craving for riches and adventure which in 1879 drove a small group of prospectors over the Continental Divide from Leadville, the second largest city in the brand-new state of Colorado. The mountains around this lost and incredible meadow were filled with silver ore. The hardy miners staked claims and named their tatter-sack collection of tents and lean-to's Ute City, in backhanded honor of the Indians whose territory they were raiding.

Several months later, Aspen's first organization man, Henry B. Gillespie, arrived. Caught up by the general promise of the place, he set out immediately for Washington to ask for a post office, road, and telegraph line. Shortly thereafter, the adventurous B. Clark Wheeler, on receiving word of the remote bonanza, clambered nearly one hundred miles on snowshoes over the mountains from Leadville. Wheeler, who may have been the town's first exploiter, immediately moved the town site, changed its name to Aspen, after the graceful, fragile trees which decorated the valley, and bought some mining claims on easy credit. Then he went back to Leadville; the return trip took seven days and some of the men used long wooden slats to walk over the snow. Thus, a kind of skiing came to Aspen in 1880. Wheeler boasted fulsomely in Leadville saloons and then went east to raise money to pay for his commitments. When Gillespie returned, he and his associates

decided that they had better move ahead quickly and by the summer of 1880 they were rolling 1,000-pound balls of ore down the mountainside in cowhide wraps. Donkey trains slowly, slowly transported the ore to smelters in Leadville. Aspen (nee Ute City) was suddenly a bustling area.

But in the winter of 1880-81, heavy snow paralyzed men and energies. Thirty-five persons stayed in Aspen. Gillespie and his wife were among them. They lived in a tremendous tent which also became the social headquarters for the stunted town. From its beginnings, Aspen did not pay attention to rules and so it had a glee club and a literary society, all unlikely endeavors in a tiny, snowbound mining camp. The beginnings of culture—in the roughest possible surroundings.

By 1883, there were 700 people in Aspen and they were, for the most part, a stable lot. Gillespie had interested Jerome B. Wheeler (no kin to B. Clark), the president of Macy's in New York, in Aspen. Wheeler was the third man to have big, definite ideas about this remote, beautiful, and rich place. He became its first benefactor.

Aspen was right on top of a rich silver lode. Some of the mines produced so much silver that they became world-famous. In 1883, a tremendous cache of ore was found in the Spar mine (for which Aspen's famous ski run, Spar Gulch, is named) and shortly thereafter the Washington, Vallejo, and Emma became bonanzas, too. An area no larger than a bedroom in the Emma netted its owners half-a-million dollars. By the end of 1884, bigtime mining began. Aspen's present-day night-time descent of the mountain in which hundreds of skiers weave through the dark with torches is a linear descendant of the nineteenth century miners winding down the steep, narrow footpaths with lanterns after a brutal

day's work. Electric tramways, an obvious forerunner of chairlifts, replaced Gillespie's crude oreballs to carry the precious stuff down to the valley floor. Actually, nearly every ceremony or spectacle in modern Aspen has its nineteenth century counterpart.

The Mollie Gibson mine became famous for its high-grade ore and further enlarged the fortunes of D. H. Hyman of Cincinnati and J. B. Wheeler. There was more high-grade ore in Aspen's mines than in any other area of the world. One 2,600-pound nugget removed from the Smuggler was 93% pure silver and had to be cut into three pieces to be moved. J. B. Wheeler built a smelter in 1884 at the junction of the Roaring Fork and Castle Creek, just west of the town, but it was not large enough to handle the ever-increasing avalanche of ore. Much had to be shipped out by pack train and wagon to distant smelters; the cost was exorbitant and ate into profits.

But in 1887, the Denver and Rio Grande railroad laid a narrow gauge spur track to Aspen from Glenwood Springs; in 1888, the Colorado Midland brought a standard broad gauge track through the Continental Divide, tunnelling through to the head of the Frying Pan River valley, traveling down that valley to Basalt and then back up to Aspen. After many colorful confrontations with rifles and sledge hammers, disputes over rights were settled and each railroad served a different side of town. The fact that two railroads would go to such lengths to get a piece of Aspen's action is indicative of its potential as a mining center.

By 1889, the mines were producing $10 million a year. The city had a population of 8,000, ten churches, three daily papers, a telephone exchange, waterworks, two railroads, free home mail delivery, a county courthouse, and thirty-three lawyers. Even today, in the midst of its new boom, Aspen has not returned to that zenith

of success. It has a population of 2,081, five churches, two weekly newspapers, a telephone exchange, a water- works, no railroads (but three scheduled airlines), no home mail delivery, a county courthouse, and twenty- six lawyers. However, retail sales (which do not by any means include all Aspen revenues) topped $25 million in 1968. Fewer people but more money. Time and pragmatism have seen fit to reverse the order of things in Aspen.

Aspen was the first town in Colorado to have electric street lights and one newspaper wrote, "Now no town of its size in the state can boast a finer class of inhabitants or better society." Restaurants served rare delicacies shipped in from both coasts. People got their clothes from New York and Paris and built "handsome and artistic residences." In these areas, nothing has changed. Ever since its resurgence, Aspen has attracted the rich and the famous, along with the poor and obscure. Hollywood stars, Supreme Court justices, busi- ness leaders, social lions mix on the slopes and in the restaurants with ski club members from Texas and Chicago and ski bums from California and New York.

The best theatrical companies on the Silver Circuit played in the Wheeler Opera House, built by J. B. Wheeler. Today the Opera House, which was gutted by a fire and restored in the 1940's and re-restored in the 1960's, features first-run films and an occasional live opera or Lions Club variety show. Wheeler also built the Hotel Jerome. It cost $165,000 and had its own greenhouse. It opened in 1889 with a grand ball which one enthusiastic newspaper reporter compared to a festi- val in ancient Rome. The Jerome chef was brought all the way from Paris. Several Parisian chefs enrich life for gourmets in modern Aspen.

On the seamier side of the mining town, there were constant street fights and duels and ladies of the

Schubert Quintette --
OF CHICAGO.
Male Quartette and MISS HUGHES, Harpist.

WHEELER OPERA HOUSE,
THURSDAY, MARCH 26, 1896.

This Ticket And 75c Will Secure You a RESERVED SEAT at
PERRY'S BOOK STORE.

250
Parquet
250
Exchange this Ticket with 75 cts for reserved seat.

evening plied their trade from cribs on Durant Avenue. Thus did gentility and the frontier meet and co-exist on the banks of the Roaring Fork. Today, Durant Avenue is lined with expensive condominiums and the last duel was arranged in 1958 (when calmer minds intervened, it was cancelled). Street fights, too, have diminished in both ardor and color. Recently, an outraged shop-keeper turned his hose on some hippies who were taking their ease on his wall. And a snowball fight escalated into a mini-riot with everyone involved taking everyone else to court for damages. More straight-forward, the miners started and finished their arguments in the streets.

In 1891, only twelve years after its founding, Aspen had a population of 11,000 and was not only the greatest silver camp in the world, but the leading commercial center between Denver and Salt Lake City. Today, Aspen—with a year-round population of 2,000 —will accommodate over 12,000 people, but its importance as a commercial center has declined. The primary business of Aspen is now pleasure. The bottom dropped out of Aspen's boom in 1893 when silver was demonitized. By dint of incredible effort and cooperation, Aspen still had 2,000 miners working in 1897. New mine shafts were cut and old ones were reworked. However, floods in the mines and the harshness of the country and the weather made the brave struggle a futile one. Mine owners finally abandoned their properties. Grass grew tall at mine entrances. People left for new lives and new opportunities elsewhere. The glory and the glamour faded away and by the 1930's there were only about 600 people living in Aspen. Many of them were old miners, dreaming forlorn dreams of the good old days, but others were young people who were having a love affair with the place.

They were attracted by its innate vigor, its singu-

larity, its strangeness, its isolation, and its beauty. Others were attracted by its potential as an outstanding ski area. In the late 1930's, a group of sportsmen became interested in tapping this potential and creating a ski resort. But World War II stymied them and the group lost most of its impetus when one of its most enthusiastic members, Billy Fiske, was killed in action while flying with England's Royal Air Force. However, the war also offered a bonus: the famed Tenth Mountain Division was sent to train at Camp Hale near Leadville. Many members of the Tenth visited Aspen, fell in love with it, and returned after the war. For all its lost fortunes, Aspen had not lost its magic. Among those who returned was Friedl Pfeifer, an Austrian who had left the Sun Valley Ski School to serve in the U. S. Army. He immediately began making plans for a ski operation.

Almost simultaneously, Chicago industrialist Walter Paepcke and his wife, looking for a site for a summer cultural center, came to Aspen. They too were struck by the enduring magic of the town and the majesty of the country.

Walter Paepcke was a resolute and audacious man. He turned a small family company into America's leading packaging firm, Container Corporation of America. That done, he began immediately to look for new and different challenges. More than anyone else, he gave Aspen its second chance at good times.

A medium-sized, sharp-featured man with calm, blue eyes, who always looked a little awkward when he smiled, Paepcke moved quietly about Aspen—usually dressed in tweed coat, sports shirt, and flannel trousers —tending to his properties, his projects, his visions. There was something outsized about both the man and his dream, but the character of the dream was always easier to analyze than the character of the man.

He made decisions quickly, he spoke with assurance, and he always kept a little distance between himself and most of the townspeople. Like many men of power and influence, he was more comfortable with other men of power and influence than with the citizenry.

Paepcke was his own best customer, faithfully attending concerts (special chairs for the Paepcke family were perpetually reserved at the Aspen Amphitheatre), lectures, and other events that he had masterminded. He hewed to his own idea that "cross-fertilization," the interplay of all kinds of ideas and cultural experiences, was vital in the development of "the whole man."

Robert Hutchins, an old friend and cultural ally of Paepcke, former chancellor of the University of Chicago, and now head of the Center for the Study of Democratic Institutions, said, "He saw [Aspen] first as a ghost town worth preserving as such. He then became interested in its possibilities for recreation. Then he began to think about it as an American Salzburg." But, as a businessman, Paepcke knew that the faded town needed an economic base and so he moved simultaneously on the economic and cultural levels.

For fifteen years, this most uncommon man devoted at least as much energy to the restoration of Aspen as he did to the affairs of Container, pumping money and ideas into his "Salzburg" in the Rockies. His confidence in his right to do what he did never faltered. Indeed, it sometimes seemed to verge on arrogance. It was natural that his manner—cool and sure—alienated some Aspen residents. What they thought, he knew. Where they hesitated, he moved forward, seemingly unruffled by occasional community indignation, seemingly amused when —during a birthday party at the renovated Wheeler Opera House—one lady said, "To Walter P. Possible who has made everything in Aspen Paepcke."

His cultural dreams in hand, Paepcke realized that

Holden Concentrator.

2252 West Aspen, and Silver Queen.

a balance of summer and winter activities would be healthier for the town, so he joined forces with Pfeifer. They formed the Aspen Skiing Corporation, which was financed by the Paepcke family and other investors from Denver and New York. It began acquiring leases and rights-of-way on Ajax; Pfeifer began planning runs. By 1946, work had begun on the first chairlift. At the same time, Paepcke formed the Aspen Company, which leased the Hotel Jerome and other large downtown buildings (including the old Opera House) and bought much property around town. Unlike Paepcke's other Aspen enterprises, the Aspen Company was organized for profit. Its immediate aim was to acquire about 10% of all the land and buildings in the town. But characteristically, Paepcke kicked profits from the Aspen Company back into his non-profit ventures.

In a prospectus prepared to interest other investors in Aspen, Paepcke wrote, "Definite plans are underway to provide opportunities for man's complete life—to earn a livelihood, to enjoy nature and physical recreation, and to have available facilities for education." To do this, Paepcke, who, in the contemporary sense of the word, was not a rich man, needed help from foundations and philanthropists and he got it. He also got help and encouragement of another sort from long-time Aspenites Fred and Frank Willoughby, who had mining interests, storekeeper Mike Magnifico, Jerome owner Laurance Elisha, and, especially, Judge William Shaw. Like Paepcke, they enjoyed the prospect of combining outdoor sports with indoor cultural events, of doing something unique in their uniquely endowed town, of restoring Aspen's lustre. And, like him, their goal was not financial gain.

In January 1947, the refurbished Hotel Jerome opened and the world's longest chairlift began operating. Wheeler Opera House reopened and Burl Ives was the

first performer. It was no longer possible to buy a downtown lot for $5. The price rose to about $100. Artists, writers, ex-members of the Tenth Mountain Division, and ardent skiers began moving in. Among the first were Bauhaus master Herbert Bayer, novelists Carl Jonas, Luke Short, and John P. Marquand, and photographers Ferenc Berko and Patrick Henry. In 1949, Aspen's second big tent went up. Designed by Eero Saarinen, the gay and giant masterpiece cost $60,000. It was inaugurated by the dazzling Goethe Bi-Centennial Festival, organized by Paepcke. The Festival brought to Aspen such luminaries as pianist Artur Rubinstein, cellist Gregory Piatigorsky, violinist Nathan Milstein, the Minneapolis Symphony with Dimitri Mitroupulos conducting, Pulitzer Prize-winning author Thornton Wilder, Jose Ortega y Gasset on his first trip outside his native Spain, and Albert Schweitzer on his first and only visit to America. This star-studded assemblage put the town back on the map.

The Aspen Institute for Humanistic Studies and the Aspen Music Festival and School grew out of the Goethe Bi-Centennial. Both were founded and headed by Paepcke. Working closely with the University of Chicago, the Institute developed a program of readings, seminars, and lectures designed to widen the minds of businessmen. The Music Festival and School brought leading musicians to Aspen for ten weeks of concerts in the tent and for high-powered instruction to promising young music students.

In 1950, the FIS world ski championships were held on Ajax Mountain. It was a real coup for the youthful resort and brought the attention of the ski world to the upstart in the Rockies. Since then, all of the important American ski events and some World Cup events have been held on the slopes where miners toiled eighty years ago. The first ski event ever to be televised

in prime-time, the French-American Challenge Cup, was filmed in Aspen. Indeed, over the years, Aspen has become a minor television star.

In the early 1950's, the Music Festival and School achieved international prominence because of the excellence of the participating musicians on the podium and in the classroom. After a skirmish dubbed "Music vs. Manure" by Denver newspapers, in which Paepcke objected to the scheduling of a rodeo on a concert day, an unlikely dilemma at best, he and the musicians suffered a schism. Finally, it was decided, with Paepcke's blessing, that the Aspen Music Festival and School should become autonomous and the the Music Associates of Aspen, governed by a board of townspeople and musicians, was formed to run the now-famous concerts and classes.

In the late 1950's, a singularly independent man, Whipple Van Ness Jones, began his own ski area, the Aspen Highlands, up the Maroon Creek canyon. With a central building, three restaurants, a beer stube, several lodges and condominiums, an ever-enlarging network of lifts, and exciting terrain, the Highlands is larger than many entire Eastern ski areas. Shortly thereafter, Pfeifer cut himself out of the Skiing Corporation, gave up his exclusive ski school franchise on Ajax, and created the Buttermilk ski area west of Aspen. Now owned and operated by the Skiing Corporation, it, too, is a large and well-designed area, made primarily for beginners, but also used by experts. And in December, 1967, the immense $10 million Snowmass-at-Aspen area, with its own self-contained village, opened. Ajax, Highlands, Buttermilk, and Snowmass make Aspen the biggest and most colorful ski resort in the United States and one of the biggest in the world. The complex has some of the pioneer spirit of Stowe, some of the glamour of Sugarbush, some of the elegance of Sun Valley, yet it has

an identity all its own in skiers' eyes.

The Music Festival and School continues to attract first-rate musicians, talented young students, and ever-increasing audiences. And the Institute continues to present its summer lecture series and to run its round of two-week seminars for businessmen. Its first office was a broom closet off the Jerome lobby; now it has a complex of buildings, including seminar rooms, auditorium, library, gallery, and numbers of offices. Through the energies of then-executive director, Robert W. Craig, a scholarly bon vivant who had been a member of the tragic K2 climbing expedition, and program director Robert Murray, a pale, intense playwright from Madison, Wisconsin, the Institute in the 1950's—under Paepcke's supervision—and early 1960's became an active force for accomplishment in the humanities. The International Design Conference, an annual week-long meeting, was begun by the Institute and now operates autonomously. A scholar-in-residence program and the Aspen Film Conference are other Institute-sponsored projects. AIHS also inspired a parallel Physics Institute which now has its own program and buildings.

Walter Paepcke died in 1960, a victim of cancer at the age of sixty-three, his work unfinished and Aspen in midstream. History will judge him favorably. If he had lived, Aspen might not have become an unwilling victim of developers. Walter Paepcke was not a developer. He was a patron. He wanted not profits from Aspen, but prominence for Aspen as a cultural-recreational center. It was not his methods that occasionally incurred wrath from townspeople, it was his overwhelming belief that he was the only person capable of making Aspen's big decisions. The irony is that he may have been right.

Robert O. Anderson, now chairman of the board of the Atlantic-Richfield oil empire, succeeded Paepcke

as president and, ultimately, chairman of the board of the Aspen Institute. Anderson, a smooth, complex man of wide financial and aesthetic interests, established and funded the annual $30,000 Aspen Award which is given to persons of accomplishment in the humanities. He and his wife gave the Music Associates its pleasant, sylvan campus outside Aspen on Castle Creek. He recently gave the Aspen Historical Society $50,000 toward the purchase of the Stallard House, a mansion the Society has converted to a museum. He has given a large sum of money to the Institute.

Like Paepcke, Anderson has been generous to Aspen. Like Paepcke, he is a patron, not a developer. Unlike Paepcke, he is not interested in playing a leading role in the affairs of Aspen. Most of his land holdings have been turned over to the Institute. He personally owns some business property in downtown Aspen, two large houses in the west end (one of which was recently put up for sale), and a lumber and supply company, not the holdings one might expect a captain of industry to list in a boom town where he has had major power for fifteen years. Anderson says (and his actions have borne him out) that he is not interested in exercising either power or influence in Aspen. Nor is he interested in increasing the involvement of the Institute in community affairs. It began as a small and exclusive cultural enclave and has remained small and exclusive. In twenty years, a mere 2,000 executives have participated in its seminars. This lack of growth is no accident. Bigness may be a virtue in bank rolls, factories, and business. But smallness is a virtue (when combined with exclusiveness) in business barons' clubs, watering holes, and cultural endeavors. Not only has the Institute deliberately not grown with Aspen, but it has just as deliberately turned its back on the *sturm*

und drang associated with that growth.

Quiet, charming, enigmatic, Anderson is probably one of America's richest men. There is no question that he knows and understands the uses of power. If he had wished to, he could have—during his decade at the head of the Institute—profoundly affected Aspen's development. But he did not wish to. He says that he has stayed out of Aspen's affairs because he had no wish to engage in "personality clashes" and because he felt that the townspeople might have resented "outside interference."

Robert O. Anderson's era in Aspen and at the Aspen Institute has been notable, like the man itself, for its quiet. Under Anderson and William Stevenson, recently retired president of the Institute and president-emeritus of Oberlin College, the Institute traded its energetic community role for a kind of intellectual withdrawal, its civic commitment for alliances with outside foundations and academic organizations. Though its credentials as a viable educational and cultural institution may have become more impressive in the last several years, its role in Aspen has become somewhat mysterious. Residents seem perpetually unsure as to what is actually happening at the Institute. Little appears in either of the local papers about its activities. This aura of mystery has compounded the Institute's alienation from Aspen.

Joseph E. Slater, ex-president of the Salk Institute, former Ford Foundation official, and, briefly, Deputy Assistant Secretary of State, became president of the Institute on March 1, 1970. He recommended a "sharing of talent" and "more effective communication" between the Institute and Aspen's other cultural-educational entities. Beyond that, there is apt to be no change in the Institute's aloof stance. It will remain elite and exclusive, small and special, a serene island,

lending a cultural patina to Aspen, but denying it the philosophical leadership which many townspeople have missed and longed for since the death of Walter Paepcke.

In the decade since Paepcke's death, other leaders have emerged in Aspen. D. R. C. Brown, son of one of Aspen's founding citizens, runs the Aspen Skiing Corporation, though the bulk of the stock is held by Mrs. Paepcke's brother, Paul Nitze, a former Deputy Secretary of Defense. Architect Fredric Benedict, one of the Tenth Mountain Division emigres, has helped shape Aspen's zoning codes and through his design office has helped create the look of modern Aspen. *Aspen Times* editor and publisher William R. Dunaway is an outspoken and forceful man whose editorials regularly reap praise and awards from liberals and scorn and abuse from conservatives. Doctor Robert Barnard, long active in city politics and civic affairs and two-term mayor, is equally outspoken and forceful and receives equal amounts of praise and censure, often from Dunaway. Pitkin County Commissioners Doctor J. Sterling Baxter, Tom Sardy, a businessman, and Clyde Vagneur, a rancher, have considerable clout, as do County Attorney Robert Delaney (who lives in Garfield County) and retired Commissioner Orest Gerbaz. Most of these men are in their forties or older and, as yet, younger leaders have not emerged. Sardy, Barnard, Dunaway, and Brown are abrasive, strong men who go full speed ahead when they think they are right. Younger men in positions of authority are smoother, blander, and warier. It may be that the gritty independence that has always marked Aspen's leaders is on its way out.

III

Modern Aspen, with its mining camp heritage, has a strong legacy of adventure and uncut beauty, but no ancient fetishes, goblins, or curses. There are signs of

the past everywhere, but there are no impositions of the past on the present. In some small towns in America, tomorrow is precisely defined by today's and yesterday's generations. Not in Aspen. In most small towns, young people leave when they reach the age of dissent. Since 1945, young people have swarmed into Aspen. There is a generation gap in Aspen, but it is not quite so wide as in other places. Indeed, something far more worthwhile than static custom and ceremony is handed on in Aspen. It is the right to be one's self. As one elegant, middle-aged lady who moved to Aspen from Chicago over twenty years ago said, "After all, we are all hippies. We all came here," she went on in precise syllables, "to do our own thing, didn't we?" Aspen's free-wheeling atmosphere has long attracted individualists. The men who founded it in the nineteenth century and the men who brought it back in the twentieth century share the qualities of independence, energy, and irreverence. As much as greed, an appetite for adventure whipped Aspen's first residents over the Continental Divide. Their descendents, natural and adopted, have that same lust.

Impressed by both nature and history, Aspen—in this super-organized and stratified world—is still a bastion of disorganized, unstratified life. In Aspen, the norm is off-center. And it is that fact that drives the money men up the walls. The usual arguments about growth and progress simply do not interest many Aspen residents. They work hard, but many refuse to take permanent jobs, working only long enough and often enough to keep themselves afloat. They wash dishes, hammer nails, sell books until they have a little money saved. Then they quit, live as they like till the money runs out, and then take another short-term job. Getting ahead is not on their minds.

However, as Aspen succeeds, the conflicts of interest

escalate. Heavy snows mean a big winter for the skiing corporations and tourist-oriented businessmen. But heavy snows mean a bitch of a winter for ranchers whose cattle become fatally ensnared in the white. Success means publicity and publicity means more success and more success means more people—all things that many Aspen residents do not regard with enthusiasm. On eying last year's Christmas throngs, one resident said, "Where did we go wrong?" More recently, at a town meeting, one man suggested that a sign reading FULL be put up at the city limits.

Aspen—with its vast expanse of ski runs and snow bowls, its unusual shops, its first-rate restaurants, its nightclubs—is a nearly peerless ski resort. Aspen is an unmatched conglomerate of culture and rough-and-ready outdoors. Aspen is world-renowned. Aspen is a smash hit. Residents who lived precarious lives ten years ago are actually making money. And some of them don't like it.

But until recently, few people came to Aspen to get rich. The natives and the new old-timers, having scratched and scrimped to make do, have a legitimate basis for their outrage at the invasion of the late-blooming money men. They feel that they made the place and now the newcomers want to destroy it. For money.

Aspen's city fathers are caught between yesterday and tomorrow, between the idealists and the pragmatists. Their awkward stance in the middle ground makes local politics boisterous, baffling, and occasionally manic. During the last ten years, everything has skyrocketed—from retail sales to skier days to problems.

There was a time when Aspen City Council meetings were placid and meandering affairs, marked by humor, good fellowship, and calm. Now council meetings are possessed by a tense urgency and are often disrupted by shouting matches. Sometimes the idealists

and the pragmatists shout at each other, while the city fathers look on with a marked lack of enjoyment. At other times, the fathers themselves participate in the shouting. Between battles, they supervise an increasingly complicated set of municipal machinery. More and more professionals have been pressed into service to do the jobs that amateurs used to do easily and capably. The city administrator is paid a larger annual salary than the mayor of Denver (population: 500,000).

Politics in Aspen—like everything else—are atypical, confused, and shot through with contrariness. Voter registration rolls show more Independents than Republicans or Democrats. The town is certainly liberal in spirit, yet only once in the last fifteen years has it given a majority to a liberal Presidential candidate and that year Barry Goldwater was the alternative. There seem to be more active Republicans than Democrats at caucus time. But, essentially, party labels mean very little. City elections are non-partisan, but that does not diminish the ardor of the contests. Old-timers often refuse to support other old-timers. Newcomers change allegiances daily. Personal and unpolitical feuds play key roles. Language invariably gets very ripe as the election approaches. The post office is awash in sensational mimeographed mailing pieces in which the candidates have at each other. Secret investigations of candidates' past behavior are not unknown. Men run together on the same ticket—e.g., "The Clean Sweep"—and then, on achieving office, turn on each other bitterly and noisily.

Some people are offended by the circus atmosphere of Aspen politics. But it is actually very much in character with the nature of the place. One should simply not expect to find tea party manners in Aspen's political arena.

So the idealists and the pragmatists have at each other and yesterday collides with tomorrow all over

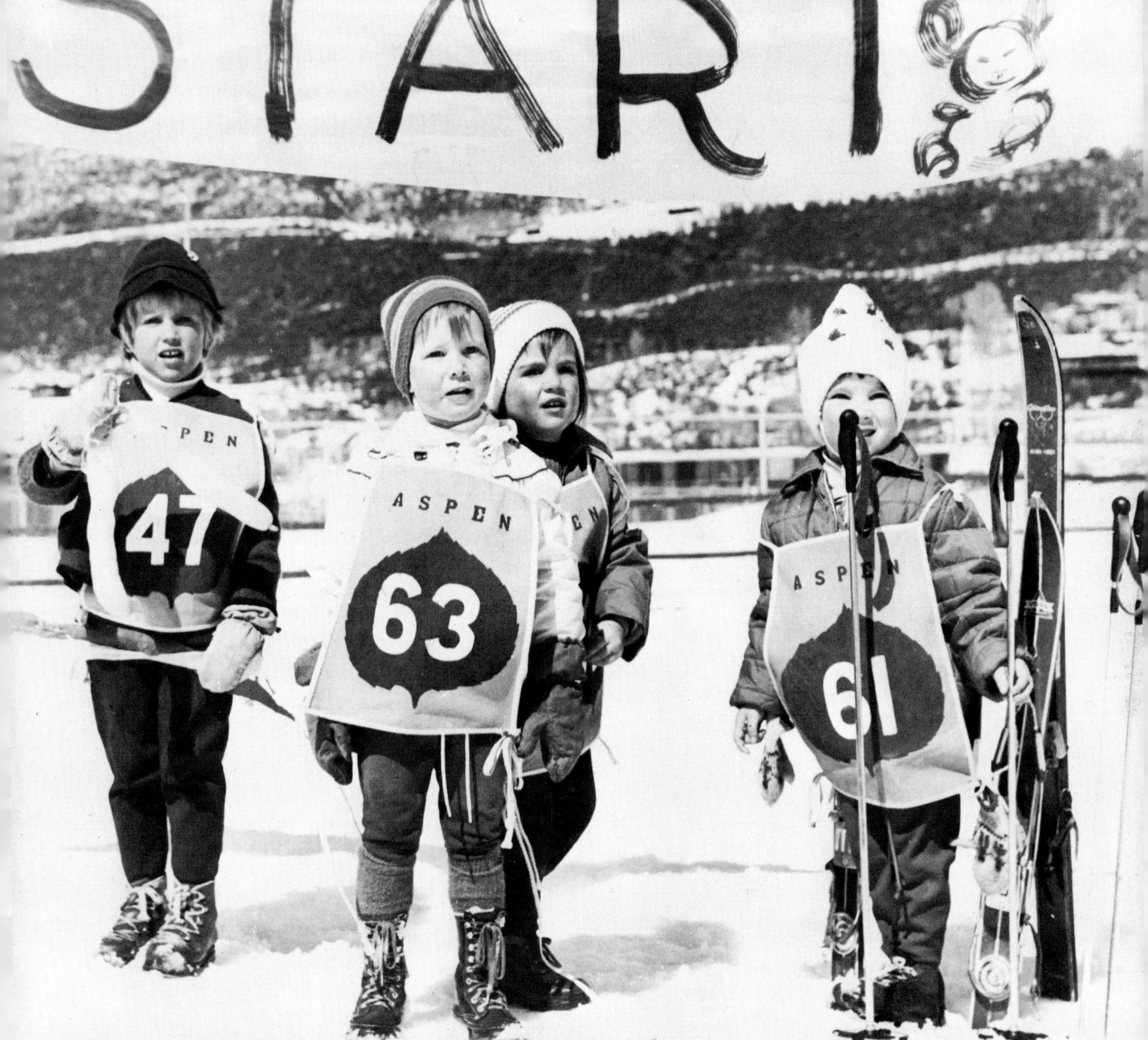
START
ASPEN
47
ASPEN
63
ASPEN
61

Aspen and the city fathers occupy a perpetual hot seat somewhere in the middle, alternately accused of being sell-outs, dictators, and, on some occasions, morons.

In ever-increasing numbers, the ambitious and the avaricious gravitate to Aspen. Well-insulated against magic and completely insured against an accident of wonder, they see a cockeyed town of 2,000 people buried in the Rockies, 200 miles from anywhere, which has somehow become one of the most popular watering holes in America. They see the beauty parts—the freedom, the excitement, the drama of the seasons, the immensity of the landscape, the rich stew of people —but they respond only to the dollar signs. It's a gold mine and they want to be in on it. And so they move in with their money and their big plans. The money men, if they are allowed to take over in Aspen, may accomplish what tragedy, disaster, and fifty years of bad times couldn't accomplish: they may destroy Aspen.

More than anything else, Aspen is people and many of those people are stubborn, sublime, idealistic, old-fashioned eccentrics. More than the mountains or the sky or the snow or the music, they are what Aspen is all about.

Chapter 3 / The People

From the beginning, Aspen's people have been pioneers. In the 1880's, pioneers simply went West and did battle with the country, the weather, the Indians, and the other pioneers. There were immediate and tangible rewards. The man who got to the horizon first owned it. In the 1970's, the pioneer's life is more complicated. He battles with developers for his land and his vistas, he struggles with the Federal government and private industry to preserve his rivers and his forests. All of the virgin horizons have vanished. The country has shrunk. The lost places have disappeared.

Many of Aspen's residents have given up comfortable, cushioned lives in the cities and suburbs and learned new skills. Their tools and their goals are often intangible and therefore indefensible in this materialistic society. They are dismissed as dreamers, escapists, or anachronisms. Dean William Birenbaum of New York's New School once said, "I deplore the fact that people try to escape the city. You have to face reality, and the cities are reality. This is where the issues are acute and where solutions must be worked out, not on a Colorado mountain top."

Aspen's modern pioneers would disagree with the good dean. They face an issue today which has national significance: the problem of environmental collapse. And there is no escaping it, no matter where you go. Life today on "a Colorado mountain top" is as fraught with "reality" as life in New York's canyons. Indeed, the mountain tops may be where the battle to preserve our environment is finally won or lost.

Problems notwithstanding, Aspen's latterday immigrants moved here not so much to get away from the city as to live in a different way. It was a style of life, not a geographic entity that they left behind. A style of life that had to do with "getting ahead" and "succeeding," that had to do with "status" and "security" and two cars in the garage. These late-model pioneers saw life as something to be celebrated, not merely endured. And Aspen seemed an ideal site for the celebration. Some of them heard about Aspen through the Goethe Bi-Centennial, that intellectual spectacular. Others heard that it had great skiing. Others simply drifted in and never left. All found it was a better place than the places they'd left behind.

They came, these seekers, from all parts of America and many countries in Europe. And they stayed. They have all kinds of backgrounds—from Eastern Establishment to Southern rural, from Midwest Gothic to Far West Sun God. They express the human condition in its most extreme and various modes. But, more than anything else, they are themselves.

It was one of those tempting, but tricky spring days when we interviewed William D. Noonan, a true generalist. We talked indoors, but his eyes were outside, on a stretch of blue that was changing shape from minute to minute. Noonan, called Roof, Roofer, or Billy by his friends, has a soft, vague Southern accent, a striking blond wife, several dogs, cats, and rabbits, an ancient school bus, two acres of land on the Roaring Fork, a houseful of furniture, a new store full of old things in the Hotel Jerome, and an easy manner which masks a volcanic temper. But his most unique possession is the hard vein of independence which has shaped his life and his personality.

Whatever else Billy Noonan may be, he is independent. Neither hippie nor square, he is simply himself. Medium height, slight build, attractive, free and twenty-eight. He wears rugged clothes—corduroy and denim— most of the time, but in tweed jacket, striped tie, and flannels, he can look as correct and conventional as his businessman brother . . . except for a luxurious bush of a mustache. There seems to be little pattern to his life; for the most part, he does what he likes and simply avoids what he doesn't like to do. But in conversation, a pattern emerges and it is entirely his own and it has to do with that stretch of blue.

Q: Tell us something about your background.
I'm from Louisville, Kentucky. Upper middle class, I guess. I went to parochial schools in Louisville, then boarding school in Florida, then a year at Washington and Lee University in Virginia, then off and on for two

and a half years at the University of Louisville, majoring in business and economics.

Q: When did you first come to Aspen?

In 1962. I'd been working as a bartender at Yellowstone and I came down here for two weeks to visit some friends from Louisville. I stayed two and a half months. Then I went back to school in Louisville, spent the next summer in San Francisco, then back to Louisville, then to the Virgin Islands for two weeks. I stayed there a year and when I got tired of sand and palm trees, I came back to Aspen to stay.

Q: What was your initial reaction to Aspen?

Terrific. It stuck in my head all the time I was away. All my life the most important thing to me has been the outdoors. Hunting and fishing and hiking. When I got here, it was everything I'd always wanted. And the town was small enough so you knew everyone, but it was cosmopolitan at the same time. The combination of this country and this town really appealed to me.

Q: What jobs have you had here?

Wow! Waiter, dishwasher, photographer, darkroom technician at both newspapers. Started a small newspaper with my wife and a friend; we sold ads, did the printing and distribution, ran the business end. Then we had an antique store. We bought an old store near Marble, Colorado. It was full of antiques and junk. We figured that we could sell the old stuff to pay for the land and then keep the land as a kind of investment and maybe build a small cabin on it. So we hauled all the old stuff back here and cleaned it and rented shop space. We called ourselves the Wooden Nickel. Six weeks after we opened, a guy from New York walked in and bought the whole store . . . for twice what we'd paid for the land and we still had the land. We debated whether to buy land in Aspen or go to Europe and decided to go to Europe. We were there four months and then came

back and started all over again. Two years ago, we bought two acres on the Roaring Fork where we hope eventually to build. Now we have another antique store, Wooden Nickel the second.

Q: We gather you don't like working for wages.

That's true. I've never liked working for someone else. Punching a time clock eats at my soul, really gets to me. Spending eight hours a day in the darkroom, not knowing whether the sun was shining, seemed insane after a while. The best times I've had have been when I was my own boss. That's the reason I came here. If I'd wanted to work 9 to 5, I could have stayed in Louisville and made three times the money I'm making now.

Q: What do you do in your free time?

Hike, fish, hunt, read, sit in the sun. I don't ski. The only good people in Aspen are the people who don't ski (broad smile).

Q: What does your family think of your way of life?

They're happy if I'm happy. I had a terrific childhood. No problems at all. My parents have always known that I wasn't going into business, that I'd do something outside, something with my hands. So when I came out here, they thought it was great. My older brother went the other route. Graduated from college, got married, had two children, sold insurance, worked in advertising, and had an ulcer when he was twenty-eight. He's very much like me, but he's been caught in the mill and there's no way out now. I guess by society's standards, he's more successful than I am . . . or more normal anyway. But I'm self-sufficient. However, my parents have always been ready to help, ready to back me in anything I want to do. Daddy was in the same business for forty years, so it's hard for him to understand my moving around, changing jobs, but he's behind me anyway.

Q: What do you like about the antique business, what made you get back into it again?

Dealing with the old junk, fixing up old things, and I like traveling around and buying it, too. When I was in high school, I used to go to farm auctions. They were like parties. I really like country people. It's always been easy for me to identify with them. They have a lot on the ball, they're simple and sensitive, more honest. And they say beautiful things and have tremendous humor. And I get a kick out of taking a piece of junk that I paid 50 cents for, fixing it up, and selling it to some horse's ass for $25. There's too goddamn much money around. People will pay anything if they want something.

Q: Why did you go to Europe?

Because I'd never been there and I had the time and money and was curious. And, of course, my wife wanted to go, too. She actually did all the organizing. But we didn't have any itinerary. We just went where we felt like going.

Q: How old are you?

I can never remember. Twenty-seven. No. Twenty-eight. I was born in 1941. Old man. Grey hair.

Q: How long have you been married?

Three years.

Q: What jobs has your wife had?

God, in three years, she's probably done ten or fifteen things. Sales clerk, cocktail waitress, hostess at a restaurant, the newspaper and the stores, of course, free-lance interior decorating and design, sign-painting, logo designs. She's an artist, but she's done just about everything there is to do in Aspen.

Q: What things matter to you?

Three years ago, where I lived was more important than what I did. We want children, but not until we have our own house. Then I have a basic desire for fulfillment. I want to do something that matters, that satisfies me. Money has become more important. Aspen

is becoming a hard place to live for someone like myself. Anyone can exist here, but the only way you can make it is to work for yourself. But I prefer working for myself anyway.

Q: *Are you going to go on living in Aspen?*

Right now I'd say yes. With all the bitching and complaining I do, there's still something about Aspen, so many great things. It's still an easy place for me to live. And if I can get a house up and make my business a success then I can do the other things I want to do. Besides, I can still go out in the woods and lose myself, as if I were 1,000 miles from anywhere. But I want to get more involved in local government, too. If I'm going to raise my children here, then I have to make an effort to make Aspen a good place to live. That means getting involved. It really is a grass-roots thing. You can scream and yell, but it's action that counts and that means working from the precinct level on up.

Q: *What things bother you the most about Aspen today?*

High rents, low wages, a sort of new commercialism. It was much more relaxed three years ago. The pace is much faster now. Three years ago, you knew almost everyone you saw on the streets, now you only see the people you know in the off-season, after the crowds have left. Basically, I'm a very lazy person and it's getting harder for me to be lazy here. And river pollution, polluting my river, that bugs me.

Q: *Who or what do you think is the real villain of the piece?*

Too much money. That's all. Here and all over the country. We have no plan to deal with this massive invasion of money. Sometimes, I think I'm being stupid not to get on the bandwagon, invest in a lousy condominium, take my profits and move to Salmon, Idaho. But that kind of thing just doesn't make sense to me.

So you hang on and hope for the best and get more involved.

Q: *Are you happy?*

Here? Yes, I think so. I'm much happier than I'd be in a bank, spending my weekends at the country club. That's what I ran from. That life never appealed to me and I didn't want my children to grow up in that atmosphere. Friends of mine in Louisville tell me they admire my guts, but it was the easiest thing in the world for me to do.

89

Architect and planner Fredric Benedict lives in an incredible house with a grass roof, a waterfall, and an immense atrium on the Roaring Fork River, east of Aspen, but, at the time of the interview, his house was occupied by friends and he was in Aspen for only a few weeks, having spent most of the winter with his French-born wife and three of their four children in France. It was a spangled spring day when we talked and Benedict seemed to be enjoying the day, the interview, and the look of Aspen's west end.

An Aspen resident since 1945, Benedict has figured large in the development of the town and the valley. As an architect, he has devised a uniquely suitable style of architecture for the country and the climate, utilizing native stone and natural woods. And his buildings are everywhere. As an architect and planner, he was the designer of Snowmass-at-Aspen's West Village. As a planner and land developer, he has left his mark in almost every residential area in and near Aspen. He was also instrumental in the development of Aspen's zoning and planning codes and policies.

Benedict is a big man, tan and fit, physically imposing, but somehow vulnerable, confident, and shy all at once. And he is something of a visionary.

Q: When did you first come to Aspen?
In 1941. I was on my way from Taliesin West in Arizona to Taliesin East in Wisconsin. I had read a lot about Aspen in *Ski Annual* and I liked the mountains and the West. I really liked the sound of it. So I stopped off and the Nationals were being held. It was great. A big ski

event for Aspen and all the old miners wandering around. It was just what I expected. I even got free lodging because I had won a race in Arizona which qualified me for the Nationals. But I didn't race. I broke my skis. But I had a great time anyway. Shortly after that I was drafted, stationed at Camp Hale in Leadville with the Tenth Mountain Division, so I saw Aspen again. And then I came back after the war to live.

Q: What do you think of it now?

Well, you can't turn the clock back. Aspen has lost some of its character, but it hasn't lost the war. There are still lots of good things here and there are ways to preserve those good things.

Q: What are the ways?

Density control comes first. We must control the growth, the population explosion, and the only way to do that is to control the number of tourist beds. That means density controls. Without the controls, we might as well give up. In addition, we should go ahead and turn the central downtown shopping area into a pedestrian mall. If we make it attractive enough and make it clear that the best shops are on the mall, no one will suffer financially. But everyone's doing so well now, it'd be hard to convince them that a mall would improve things. Then, we should have a shopping center down near the river. It should be oriented more to service and basic types of businesses. Food stores and so on. That would eliminate some of the residential traffic in the downtown area, relieve some of the congestion. And the city should undertake, perhaps with the help of private citizens, to buy up and preserve open space around the town, especially the downtown area. This land not only could be used immediately for parking but would guarantee permanent preservation of open space for view and prevent further building congestion. If we did those four things—density control, malls,

shopping center away from the middle of town, preservation of open space—we'd make big strides in retaining Aspen's character. The developers have no foresight. They can't see that if they go on building and building at the present rate they'll destroy the very thing that makes Aspen popular and successful as a resort and a good place to live. If they can't see it themselves, then they have to be controlled.

Q: How many people can Aspen hold, residents and tourists?

It's already all out of balance. In Europe, ski resorts—which are now completely planned like Snowmass and Vail—decide at the beginning how many people the mountain can hold and then they base all their planning and building on that figure. But people have a way of fooling the planners. Snowmass estimates that their combination of mountains will accommodate 17,000 people. So they'll base their building on that figure. But people will come there from down the valley and other residential areas in the vicinity of Snowmass. Perfect planning is impossible, but we have too many tourist accommodations in Aspen right now. It has occurred to me, however, that as the new accommodations go in, the older ones will perhaps become permanent housing for locals. In fact, the Aspen Skiing Corporation has bought an apartment building for use by employees. If that happens on a larger scale, things will become somewhat more balanced. But we still need density controls. And strict ones.

Q: Is Aspen in danger of becoming a sort of "inner city," at the mercy of its satellites?

Aspen is the center of the action in the Roaring Fork Valley. And it will continue to be. The best shops, best nightclubs, best restaurants are here. It should accept its role as what someone called "the hub of it all" and plan for that, too, because it means that the action

is going to continue to be concentrated here. We can't abdicate from the role, whether we want to or not, but we can plan for it. That's one of the reasons the mall and the shopping center would be good moves.

Q: Could anything have been done, anything substantial, years ago, to prevent this accelerated growth now?

If the county had not been so eager to get tax delinquent lots on the tax rolls, there would now be blocks of land for parking, green space, etc. When I moved here, hundreds of city lots were being sold for $10 or $15 apiece. Now they are worth up to $30,000 apiece. If Walter Paepcke had bought more land along the bottom of the mountain years ago, we might have had more control, preserved more green space, been able to plan more efficiently. But Vail's owners had complete control and they will grow beyond an ideal size. Maybe there isn't any way to really control a successful area. Except maybe a benevolent dictatorship. And of course, there are all the greedy land developers like myself around to take advantage of the situation. (laughter)

Q: When was the turning point in Aspen?

It seems to me that it must be related to skier days. When they began climbing, things began happening. I think that the condominiums have only been a big thing for three or four years, But, of course, the bank was the first thing done by outsiders on a big scale. And that was 1961. It's been building pretty fast ever since then, I guess.

Q: What will happen if the accelerated pace continues?

Aspen is a lodestone now. But in five years, Snowmass will have all that Aspen has in the way of apres-ski life and conveniences and excitement. Sophisticated skiers will be more inclined to go to a place like that than an overcrowded town like Aspen. Skiers nowadays like convenience and comfort and they'll have that and excitement, too, at the planned resorts. It could easily happen that the newer resorts with gentler slopes, more sun, and ability to ski from one's doorstep will take over from the older places. It's already happening in Europe. Some hotels in Chamonix actually close in January. It is simply much easier for a skier to get what he wants in a controlled resort with pyramided organization—like Sun Valley or Vail.

Q: But some people think controlled resorts are deadly dull, inhuman.

Not necessarily. Good planning is not evil, it's sensible. When you plan a community, you can at least avoid some of the hazards of rapid growth and you have more opportunity to establish and maintain good atmosphere and high standards. We just can't hold onto our small towns and their values anymore. New towns, carefully planned and controlled, have a much better opportunity to offer a setting for the good life. And a limit can be placed on the town's size.

Q: You have been both a planner and architect and a land developer. Do you see any conflict of interest?

Well, I may be prejudiced, but I think when you get down to the nitty-gritty, it's better to have an architect involved in land development than not.

Q: You've designed all kinds of buildings, you've planned residential areas and now you're—with Snow-mass—totally involved in the design and planning of a complete community. Will you continue to work more in design/planning than in pure design?

Yes. I think architects should get more involved in social—as well as aesthetic—problems. And there is certainly more satisfaction in more involvement. I own some land east of Aspen, and a parcel out near Snow-mass. I will someday plan, design, and develop those areas myself and then I can really experiment with new concepts, because they will be entirely my projects.

Q: Could you tell us some of your ideas, some of the things you'd like to do?

Well, there are lots of things. I was talking today to some Yale architectural students about some land I own near Ruedi. We were talking about carving cave-like rooms into the gypsum cliffs there. And then using the leftover gypsum—as plaster of paris—to make other forms and spaces. I'm not sure whether it'll work, but we're going to try it. Then I'd like to build some sort of arts center on my land east of town, some sort of complex where people in various fields could do their work. Painters. Potters. Photographers. Maybe even scientists. And I've been thinking about an idea for a big new town, maybe on Federal land in Utah, where the climate's good and the blacks and the young could be in on the ground floor and really have an important role in the town. I think it's silly to rebuild the ghettos. Rebuilding won't change the conditions that surround the ghettos. I think we need new towns where the residents would create their own market. I mean, it would sustain itself. Then I've also been thinking of building a residential community, sort of an old-fashioned neighborhood, which would have nothing to do with tourists or tourism, a place with perhaps nothing more commercial than a general store and a post office.

Q: Where would you build it?

I really don't know. Perhaps on Hunter Creek land I own. I hadn't really wanted to do anything with that land until the McCulloch Oil Company bought adjacent land. I wanted to see the valley remain a roadless wilderness. When and if McCulloch develops, I will probably do something with my land, because the wilderness character will be gone.

Q: You have lots of ideas about the future, new towns, planned resorts, but what about now, what about the small towns in the midwest and the small farms?

The Federal government decided twenty years ago that they should try to eliminate marginal farms, because they were inefficient. In the Ozarks and Appalachia. That was a mistake. The farm subsidies should have been structured to encourage people to stay on the land. But they left the land and went to the cities. Now there's a surplus of empty houses in the country, the small towns have lost their economic base, and the population of the cities is soaring. If the government had only acted years ago, had restructured the subsidies, they could have kept the rural areas alive. It's happening in France, too. Villages are dying, people are leaving the farms to go to the cities. But we still have many small farms and something should be done to save them and the way of life they represent. It's a much bigger problem than what's happening to Aspen. It's too bad some of those little towns couldn't develop resort facilities. You know in three or four years jumbo jets will be able to carry so many people so far so fast that the Aspens of the world will be overwhelmed.

Q: Are you optimistic about the future—yours and Aspen's?

I am very pessimistic about life in large cities; they can only become less livable. This means more people trying to escape to places like Aspen. At the moment there is little reason to be optimistic that Aspen can withstand this kind of pressure. Aspen has always been very divisive. Unless there is a pulling together by the newspapers, elected officials, the various organizations, and the general populace, there is little chance for achieving common goals. The recognition of the need to hire a full-time planner is a hopeful sign.

Q: Would you be happy living in a planned community?

Yes. By a planned community, I visualize a pedestrian

one where it is possible to take a pleasant walk to most places where one wants to go. The automobile must be convenient when needed but not so obvious, overpowering, and omnipresent as it is in communities that were not planned for it. Planned communities, by nature, have a contrived, company town character at first but as time goes on, they should develop a natural vitality common to towns that just grew. I think this naturalness can be achieved more rapidly by giving importance to the people who work in the community—offering a place for everyone to live there instead of forcing them to commute. For example, build apartments above or behind shops for the shop owners.

Q: What was your favorite year?

For at least twenty years, every year has been better than the others. So my best year has yet to arrive.

Folksinger, writer, photographer, and self-proclaimed river rat, Katie Lee was in the midst of some frenzied spring-cleaning project when we arrived at her small Victorian house near the busy center of Aspen to interview her. The house seemed immaculate in the clear sunlight, full of things she had collected in her travels and photographs of the Southwest country she loves. Her feeling for the rivers and the wilderness shone out of those large photos.

Wearing a peculiar hat of pastel feathers, a white shirt, and green slacks, drinking coffee and eating wedges of toast lustily, Miss Lee looked more like an eccentric housewife than the worldly-wise lady who appears on her record jackets. She is a small, spare woman who does everything with a kind of intensity that is rare in this era of super cool, but especially rare in a fifty-year-old woman. Sometimes profane, sometimes forlorn, she is angry at the world most of the time, yet she seems to enjoy life immensely.

She knows what she thinks and she says what she thinks, making no effort to be coy or politic. There is one very important thing about Katie Lee: she gives as good as she gets.

Q: What's your background?
I was born in Tucson in 1919. My mother and father were contractors and designers. We'd build a house and then several others and then move on. My dad was a dreamer; my mother was practical. She held things together. Because of the business, I lived on almost every street in Tucson sooner or later. My mother and

I were very conscious of houses. We'd walk into a house, look around, and if we didn't like the vibrations, we'd get out. My parents were divorced when I was thirteen. Then my mother went into real estate.

Q: Did you mind moving around?

No. I don't think that children mind that kind of thing.

Q: What's your educational background?

I got my degree at the University of Arizona. Major in drama. Minor in English. And I can't spell. I don't understand why the educational system is such that three-fourths of the children can't spell. Of course, the language is all screwed up.

Q: When did you come to Aspen?

In the summer of 1959 Glen Yarbrough asked me to come sing at the old Limelite. I stayed two months. That's what turned me onto Aspen. Then in 1961 I came back to sing at the Abbey and in 1962 I moved my boat out here and in 1963 I moved into this house.

Q: And before that?

I was married and living in New Jersey and two things came clear to me. One, get out of New Jersey. Two, get rid of the man. In 1961, I moved to Denver, but I was on the road most of the time.

Q: What are you doing now?

I've been struggling all year to find a job here, but they don't use my kind of singing any more. So during the winter I sang for the sleighride parties at Snowmass. They were groovy. I had a captive audience and they wanted to hear songs about the West. And I could talk to them and tell them what it's all about. We often talked about Aspen and what's happening.

Q: Of your various occupations—writer, singer, photographer, actress—which do you most enjoy?

People say that artists are never satisfied. I did one thing till I got tired of it. Then did something else. And so on. After I had accomplished the things in a

field that I set out to do, the field became less than interesting. Now I'm fluctuating between singing and writing. Singing has gotten to the point where it's just a big drag because of the way audiences have become over the years since television was invented. They're such undisciplined, know-nothing people now because, thanks to TV, they think they are connoisseurs of art and entertainment. They didn't know anything to begin with and TV certainly didn't help them. Besides, nobody listens anymore. So I want out of it in the worst way —unless I can do concerts.

Q: How many record albums have you made?
Six.

Q: You mentioned a recent interest in writing . . .
Yes, I've done a book. It's the stories of the West that I learned from the cowboys. Little anecdotes. And songs that I've collected, from sources all over the West. I'll bet there aren't three songs in the book that anyone's ever heard of. The book reveals a few pertinent things about cowboy music which aren't generally known: that it came a lot later than most people think, that it derived from a form that suited the country perfectly—the breadth of the land, the gait of the horses and cows, the size of it all, that it's the only truly indigenous music, in my opinion anyway. They used to take lullabies and Irish jigs and alter them to suit their way of life. The book's name is "10,000 Goddamn Cattle" and it's about the complete and utter destruction of the cattle ranches and the West and why we can't do anything about it—thanks to the population explosion, which is at the bottom of all of the evils which confront us. There's nothing else we need to do but get rid of half of us. That's all. Strange how the cowboy's attitudes fit with the revolution that's going on now. They were rebels. They came out here to find the things they wanted. They were the last great individuals. Since

then, there ain't been nuthin'.

Q: Well, your aim then. . . .

After the book comes out, I want to do lecture tours
with singing, where I can get that balance that people
on the right track have. Our intuitive sense ought to
be balanced by our integrity and intelligence. Most
people don't develop both sides. They're one-sided.
People in balance are beautiful. Gradually, the physical
and the mental sides have begun to balance in me.
Now if my body doesn't fall apart . . . All our greats
are in balance. The minute I'm limited and can't get into
another field and phase, it's like somebody put the lid
on and there's a nest of wildcats under there, trying
to get out. I know that I'm too much of a performer
to really stop. I thought maybe I could, as I got older
and tireder, but I don't seem to get tired. When I go,
I don't want anybody to have anything left to take.
Like Zorba. Living is so terribly important because we
have such a little bit of time to do our thing.

Q: You worked in television, didn't you?

I worked on three shows for three years at NBC—but
that's when it was live—as an actress and a musician.
Even then, all the elements were wrong. You'd trip
over a cable in the middle of a love scene. Or the
cameraman would shout a direction in the middle of
a scene. About that time, Burl Ives came to town and
he said, "Why don't you get the hell out of this town.
It's no place for you to be singing folk songs." And
I'd been doing running parts in "Gildersleeve" and
"Halls of Ivy" and "Railroad Hour," acting and singing, and all that time the stars were sabotaging me.
When it finally hit me, I went home and cried for
three days.

*Q: I would think that the lot of the entertainer would
be simpler in our affluent society than ever before.*

It well might if TV hadn't been invented. Music used

to be an art form. Now you hear it when you're buying beans in the market, on elevators, on airplanes—when you fly to Hawaii, you hear "I've Got a Feeling I'm Falling" followed by "How Deep Is the Ocean"—whether you like it or not. It ceases to be anything at all. When you're music-oriented and you hear this watered-down junk every day, day after day, it's enough to just drive you out of your mind. I've threatened to get off of airplanes, I've thrown bottles, it makes you act like a nut. And I'm not a nut and I know it. I know who the nuts are all right. But the people are so inculcated with this that it desensitizes them to other things that are going on around them. They're shot. Their brains are not in tune with music for music's sake. They don't know the difference between noise and music. Again, it goes back to the fact that there are too many people.

Q: But don't people use music to cover other noise or to fill the quiet?

Of course, they do. But it numbs them, lulls them, but it doesn't do them any good.

Q: What about the new music, do you like it?

I love what they're saying, the good ones, with their lyrics. The Beatles. Donovan. Leonard Cohen, people who really have something to say. Again, it's that revolt that the cowboys felt seventy-five or a hundred years ago. And I like what's happened to the music, too. It's been a long time since we've had these chord changes and these strange in-and-out weavings. I think it's neat. The other music was at a standstill. It needed reseeding.

Q: Do you think there are any rebels left over thirty?

They're all over thirty. The kids aren't real rebels. To be a real rebel, you have to know what society is, where it's going, and deliberately turn your back on it. But the kids are not individuals; they're thinking in groups. It's sad. It takes time to be an individual. But with guts, you can do anything.

Q: *What do you think about Aspen today?*

Aspen is at the point right now where I'm about ready to abandon it. If we could have a moratorium on building and say not one other condominium for five years, I might stay. When I came, Aspen offered everything —it was a cultural center, there was lots of exchange here and I could make contact with the people here. I've missed that this year. I would like to stay if there were any possible means of sustaining myself. But I won't work for a wage and there you have it. Even if I do stay, I'll move out in the valley because the town is getting so hideous.

Q: *Is the same thing happening in other places?*

We're so up tight now. And there are so many of us and we have so much spare time that every time a good place is found—like Telluride was found a couple of years ago and you should see it now, the land prices are as bad as they are here. I'm thinking maybe of moving down to Sedona. It's a kind of art center.

Q: *Where is it?*

Don't you tell anyone where Sedona is. They're ruining Baja too. Everything that I've loved and really gotten hooked on is shot now. All my rivers are gone. And they were my rivers, by God.

Q: *When did you become a river rat?*

In 1952. I saw a movie on the Grand Canyon and the river. And the moment I saw it, I knew I had to go and do the rivers. That started it. I became so fascinated that I went on other trips. That's when I collected the river songs. Then I started taking other people on trips. It just got to be a thing. We'd go on fall trips for a month and that's when we named the canyons. Twenty-five of them.

Q: *Are there any rivers left?*

Not really. You can go down the Yampa and the Green.

But Glen Canyon—if they'd left it alone—was 400 river miles of complete wilderness.

Q: You once came up with something shrewd about the Reclamation Bureau . . .

O, yes, I guess you mean when I labeled it the Wreck-the-Nation Bureau. I can't remember when I first said it. It just came to me. It was simple, that's just what the Reclamation Bureau is doing.

Q: How would you summarize what's happening in Aspen?

It's natural for a little town to bicker and argue, but a horrible outside element is influencing us all. There are too many people here making too many demands and everyone is bowing to them. I see no reason why Aspen can't stay a perfectly beautiful, solid economic city without growing one more inch. People will fight to get in here if they don't think they can. I'd love to see them get their comeuppance. No snow or a depression or something. And all the buildings empty. They're on the steam roller though. Next, I suppose McCulloch Oil Company will put the Eiffel Tower at the entrance to Hunter Creek. After all, they brought London Bridge to Arizona. If I can get some land at a reasonable price, I'll go ahead and do it, put my house on it. I want roots. I'm sick and tired of paying rent and I've never been sick of paying rent before. Do you think that's a sign I'm getting old . . . older? (laughter)

THE COWBOY

Wayne Vagneur runs a 1,400-acre ranch with his father, Sullivan. With rolling green meadows and thick stands of trees and clusters of rugged old barns and corrals, it's beautiful. It has been in the Vagneur family for generations and, outwardly, time has made few changes. It was peaceful, under a benign spring sky, the day we talked to Vagneur. We sat in the tidy, comfortable, spacious kitchen—which combines a country cheer with ultra modern appliances—in his log house. His wife and younger daughter came in and out as we talked. The older daughter was at school.

Tall, lean, laconic, Vagneur—in boots, levis, checked shirt and Stetson—is the complete cowboy, the total man of the West. His family—through ownership of land and eminence in events—has dominated Woody Creek, a ranching community near Aspen, since their arrival in 1878. Like most ranchers, he is cool, contained, and completely independent. Owning and working 1,400 acres—when most people settle for a split level and a yard full of crabgrass—gives a man a rare kind of presence. In addition, Vagneur is very good at what he does and he knows it.

Q: How long have you lived in this valley?
Since I was born. I'm thirty-nine.
Q: What was it like when you were growing up?
All ranching and farms.
Q: How big is your ranch?

1,400 acres.

Q: What major changes have you seen?

Well, everyone just wants to live here because of Aspen, the climate, and the skiing.

Q: Has the development of Aspen as a major resort changed the focus of Woody Creek?

Not really. It's still mostly ranches and homes, places to live. Of course, some of the ranches have been cut up.

Q: Do you have any feeling about this gradual loss of working ranches?

I don't think so. Every place is going to change. A lot of good things and a lot of bad things have happened here.

Q: What are some of the bad things?

Too many people, too many cars, just like everyplace else.

Q: How about the changes in Aspen itself?

It's still got the best ski hill in the world.

Q: Do you like the building boom?

Not especially.

Q: Would you prefer slower growth?

You mean quiet, orderly growth? I suppose we all would. But the developers like it the way it is. They make bucks out of it.

Q: Do you have any feeling about the ranchers who have sold out to developers? Do you think they've gone against the land?

No. Someone's going to buy it eventually. This isn't real ranching country anyway. It's harder here than down below. Some people can't make enough money off their ranching here.

Q: Why do some hold out?

Because people come along and try to steal it first. Finally, the price goes up and people sell.

Q: Does that mean that everyone's going to sell out eventually?

They just about have. Almost every ranch here has changed hands at least once.

Q: What about your 1,400 acres?

We still want to live here.

Q: If a developer offered you a very good price, would you accept and hold out a piece for yourself?

Hope to. Till we find a better place anyway.

Q: Do you think that'll happen?

Eventually, I imagine.

Q: Who—among local ranchers—still own their original big parcels of land?

Weibens, Natals, and us.

Q: Can you hold out?

As long as we want to we can.

Q: If a big development came in next to you, how would you feel?

It would make our ranch worth more money.

Q: Do you think all of Woody Creek will ultimately be developed?

I think it will.

Q: How long will it take?

Ten years I would guess. Wild guess, but that's my opinion. Right now, I don't think there's any land for sale. A lot depends on the planners. But I imagine that if someone wanted to sell now, he could find a buyer.

Q: How many cattle do you run here?

250 mother cows.

Q: What's your routine in summer?

Mostly we raise hay to feed the cows in winter.

Q: What's your average day?

In the early part of the summer, I get up not too early— 7 or 8—do a few chores, irrigate, feed the cattle, and take care of them before we put them out to pasture. From the fourth of July on, we make hay.

Q: How many bales?

Close to 20,000.

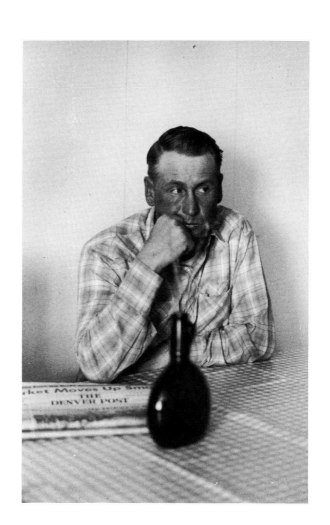

Q: How much does one weigh?

Seventy-five pounds. We use the tractor, scoop them up, make stacks, and haul some in around the buildings. That way we only have to lift them once.

Q: Is your ranch mechanized?

I've mechanized every part but that irrigating. You still have to use that shovel. Bulldozers and some other machines help, but mostly it's just as hard as it was a hundred years ago.

Q: Which part of ranching do you like the most?

Driving the cows around the hills is the best part, I guess.

Q: What is the hardest part?

Irrigating. You just have to start the water down the ditches and then get out with a shovel and scatter it.

Q: Would you rather be retired and sitting in Miami Beach than lifting 20,000 bales of hay?

I doubt that. If I retired, I wouldn't be sitting in Miami Beach.

Q: What would you be doing?

Probably riding a few horses. Skiing.

Q: How many horses do you have now?

Thirty-five.

Q: Have you skied all your life?

Somewhat. I instructed for a few years. I went two weeks ago. It was great. About two feet of fluff.

Q: Do you like Snowmass-at-Aspen?

I've never skied there.

Q: Where did you go to school?

Right here in Woody Creek. One-room schoolhouse, grades one through eight. Then I went to high school in Aspen.

Q: How many students were there in your graduating class?

Seven.

Q: On a day-to-day basis, how does Aspen and what's

happening there affect you?

It has good places to eat. My wife shops there. I do most of my business in Glenwood Springs. But when you're working hard, it doesn't make much difference what's happening anywhere except right where you are. Ranching is real independent. If you want to go home and go to bed, you go.

Q: Where do you sell your cows?

Glenwood and Rifle. We truck them down to the sales in the fall. About 150 calves a year.

Q: Have rodeos changed?

I started roping in 1945 and it hasn't changed at all. Still the same deal. A little town sponsors the rodeo. You travel around and take your chances on winning a buck.

Q: Why do you do it?

It's like any sport, it's fun. It's a thrill to be able to get on a horse and see if you can catch a steer or a calf and how quick.

Q: Is it dangerous?

Somewhat.

Q: Have you ever gotten hurt?

Slightly.

Q: Do you win?

We have.

Q: Are you in the professional league?

I wouldn't say so. Don't go to enough of them. I only get to three or four.

Q: How many Vagneurs are left on the land?

Only us.

Q: How many people work for you?

Most of the time me and one other.

Q: How do you get around in winter?

With horses and sleds. But we usually keep the cows close to the haystacks.

Q: Is a ranch this size profitable?

Enough to make a living. It was more profitable years ago, 1945-52. The price of beef was higher then.

Q: Can you make a living on a smaller ranch?

Only if you have a sideline.

Q: Do you like to put up hay?

Not too well.

Q: Have you been drastically affected by Aspen's growth, beyond the price of your land going up?

Aspen is the only place in the world where you have to stand in line to spend your money.

Q: Do you still think Woody Creek is a good place to live?

I think it is.

Q: What's the traffic like here?

Terrible. There's as much traffic on our road now as there used to be on the highway.

Q: And I imagine everybody who goes by stops?

Some days it's pretty bad. You have to go off and leave them talking.

Q: Do you like the Westerns on TV?

Some of them.

Q: Are you happy living here?

You bet. I wouldn't live here if I weren't.

Deane Billings lives in a complex of rammed earth buildings at the base of Ajax. He keeps five horses nearby in a corral. We talked to him one black spring night. He had just come back from feeding his horses and seemed relaxed and cheerful as he welcomed us into his cluttered workroom. It overflowed with the tools of his life and his work: a bass fiddle on its side, a piano, a bass mandolin, cameras and editing and projecting equipment, carpenter's and plumber's implements, and a miscellany of things he likes and needs. Right outside the door was his collection of graceful buggies and sleighs, saddles, bridles, and other equestrian gear. It was a comfortable confusion.

Billings is fifty years old and his hair is white, but in spirit he's about twenty-two. He prefers doing a little of everything rather than a lot of one thing and so he tends to his horses and his properties, occasionally plays bass in one of Aspen's nightclubs, skis joyously in season, makes films and photos, and shows a tendency to stop doing anything he becomes too successful at. Billings is gentle, strong, and funny. He is also a very formidable man.

Q: Where did you live before you came to Aspen?
I grew up in Hannibal, Missouri and St. Louis. Did graduate work and taught chemistry at Louisiana State, then I moved to Denver and taught there. I came over here in 1950.
Q: Why Aspen?
Oh, I got mixed up with the wrong crowd.
Q: What have you done since you've been here?

In Aspen, you do everything. I've been a ski instructor, bass player, photographer, carpenter, plumber. One summer I even worked in a gas station.

Q: What have you been doing recently?

Played bass with the Buffalo Hunters for a while and I've been working on a ski film, too.

Q: Tell us about the film.

I try to point out that in other sports, you make a big follow-through. Baseball pitchers, they all follow-through. Yet skiing is a short, jerky, choppy thing. That's come about because so many of our instructors have been racers. Only about one percent of the skiing populace will ever race, yet they're being taught to get down the hill in the biggest possible hurry. Most ski films are really travelogues, with the grand tour. Mine just shows that skiing can be fun. I've been working on it for about a year and have worked like hell to cut it down to fifteen minutes. Basically, it's my contribution to the sport. Joe Kloess will do an original score. I'll do the commentary. I hope to find a sponsor and maybe redo it in color. Later, I may do half-a-dozen short films on the various stages of ski technique.

Q: What things did you like about Aspen when you first arrived?

The people and the skiing.

Q: What do you like now?

The people are still here, but the skiing's gone to hell. It's our hill, but we can only use it from Thanksgiving until Christmas and then part of January. The rest of the time, you can't make a turn without looking over your shoulder to see who's about to run you down. In fact, one day up there last winter, I had the startling realization that it's no longer a ski hill, it's just a damn tourist accommodation.

Q: What do you think will happen to Aspen?

I honestly think the damn speculators are going to do it

in. I believe they have overbuilt. Eventually, Snowmass-at-Aspen will have enough attractions and, hopefully, enough atmosphere so that the goddamn people will stay out there and let us have our ski hill back. My feeling has always been that this town should never have grown beyond what was good skiing. I'd say that was about 1956 or 57 at the very latest. Whatever the number of people skiing on an average day then, that's the number the town should have been built to accommodate. To hell with Buttermilk and Snowmass, let them work their own problems out. If it had been possible for Paepcke—or Deane Billings—to have had the kind of money to have bought the whole goddamn thing and said, "All right, folks, this is the stopping point." Had we stopped in time, ultimately we'd have had something —about now—that no one else had and they'd be waiting in line to get into Aspen. If we'd just said, "This is the village, this is the ski hill—no more." Someone— Bill Cleary, I guess—said if you have a movie house and it seats a hundred people and 300 want to get in, what do you do, push the walls out and destroy the mood, the atmosphere, just to accommodate them? No, you just don't do that. You say, "We've only got a hundred seats, sorry, folks. You'll have to wait for the next showing." In the last five or six years, the outside money, speculators, absentee ownership have really begun to do the town in fast. Absentee ownership is complete speculation. Where can we make a quick buck? To me, it has spoiled the ski town atmosphere. It's just a goddamn resort now. When I first came here, someone would have a party, bring-your-own-liquor thing, because no one had a nickel and everyone in town would be there, everyone. There were always a few strays, someone's guests or something. And on the ski hill, as far away as you could see, you could tell who someone was by the way he skied. There were that few people around.

That was the great atmosphere, that was the thing that Aspen has completely lost. To me, this is the great tragedy. Had there been an infinite-sized hill, that you could go on forever and still ski the powder for two days after a good snow, instead of two hours, it wouldn't have mattered, you could still have had that atmosphere. To me, that's the great loss. I guess wherever you go, you find a certain number of friends whom you commune with rather than just know, whom you have good close rapport with. Most of them are still in town, but year by year, there are less of them. So, I guess, you cultivate a few more to replace the drop-outs.

Q: Where do they go?

Some of them move down the valley. I'm even thinking about it. For a while, I was thinking about Crested Butte. It's a delightful town. We take a five-day horseback trip over there every fall and spend a day or so, walking around looking at the old rusty roofs and the nice broad valley. I thought it might be a good place because they're never going to make it. But all of a sudden, the speculators came in and land is almost as expensive as it is in Aspen. Anyway, I went over in early April last year and it was cold and I realized that it's about 1,000 feet higher than Aspen. Spring starts too late and fall comes too early for what I'd want to do.

Q: Where are you thinking of going?

Down between Basalt and Carbondale is about it. It's about 1,500 feet lower, so I'll have a little more summer.

Q: Would you farm?

I'd play with my horses anyway. I dream of a little place there where I could look at the river, hear the chickens cackle, and watch the horses and play with them. I can still get enough skiing from Thanksgiving through February. About the first of March, it's time to start thinking about horses anyway. I still have some property where my horse corral is. So if I sold this, I'd still keep a

place here. Have to have some rental units to live on and one to live in when I wanted to be here.

Q: Is it true that someone offered you $100,000 for these two-and-a-half lots?

Yes. But I only paid about $600 for this land, so it seemed like a bad deal at the time. (laughter) They've raised the ante since then. They're getting desperate. And I think I'll probably sell. I think they'll ruin the whole thing. They've already ruined it for me. They're going to build just east of my house, about eight feet away, and across the street. It'll be so bad then that I won't even be able to get out into the traffic with my horse and buggy. When I built this mud house, the nearest neighbor was two blocks away. It was all prairie dogs and sagebrush and old junk from the mine tramway. This was a bottom terminal here and I dug into old railroad ties when I was digging my footings. And there were already a couple of old junk cars.

Q: Tell us about the mud house.

It's rammed earth. I went and gave John Herron every cent I had in the world as a down payment on this property. And I didn't have a nickel to my name. And I started building this house. As the saying goes, I didn't know it couldn't be done, so in my ignorance I went ahead and did it. Somebody gave me some old boards and I even pulled the rusty nails out of them and straightened them because I didn't have fifteen cents for a pound of nails and I made a form out of the boards. It was about three-and-a-half feet by sixteen inches by sixteen inches. After I put in the footings, I put damp earth in the form and then tamped it down to about three inches. Just went around the perimeter doing that, leaving spaces for doors and windows. It's the best way to make a wall there is.

Q: What did people think of the idea?

There were two categories of people. Half were com-

pletely astonished and the other half kept asking what would happen when it rained. After I built my house, I realized that if I built a rental unit, I could pay the taxes and the light and heat bill and I would only need money for clothes and food. But inflation always keeps that kind of independence out of reach.

Q: We heard you had a battle with the phone company. What about that?

Well, I consider the telephone a real aggravation. I'd have one and I'd have them take it out because I couldn't stand the damn thing. Then, for various reasons, I'd get another one . . . and so on. But the phone always gets out of hand. Anyway, one afternoon, I was taking a siesta, about three years ago, and I heard something on the roof and I went out in my black hat and there was this guy dragging a wire across my roof. I asked him what he was doing and he said he was putting a phone line in. I told him to get the hell off my property. Later the same day, he was back again! And I chased him off again! Then they went so far as to bury their line on my property. And I said, "I'll give you till sundown today to get that wire off my property." Well, they didn't do anything and about six weeks later I saw their trucks again. I chased one in my old stock truck and forced him onto my property and I had on my black hat and a bee-bee gun and I said to the driver, "You get the boss over here." And I chained their truck to my truck. It turned out that that was a felony. They could steal my land, but I do the same thing with their goddamn truck and it's a felony. And the other's a civil suit. So I chopped through their damn line with a spade. And I let my bill run up and told them to take the phone out for the last time. I said, "I don't ever want to catch any of you bastards on my property again." Then the district manager came and wanted to know why they couldn't put their wires across my land. After all that! Finally, they yanked their line out and I enjoyed watching them hauling it all the way around on the other side in the snow.

Q: Do you have a phone now?

No. I'll never have another phone as long as I live. One of my tenants wanted a phone and I said to him, "You don't need a phone—take it from me. If you need one that badly, you get yourself another apartment."

Q: What's your favorite thing to do?

Make love. Then skiing and horsebacking. In that order. I guess.

Q: Does Aspen still have a chance?

It's really a shame, the town going the way of the almighty dollar. It's too late for Aspen, but maybe there's a chance for some other town. The biggest mistake is to pave streets, put in sewers, other improvements. Those things just attract more people. They come here to live because they like it and suddenly they start wanting all the things they left behind. People even complain about the dust. Imagine coming from Houston to Aspen and complaining about the dust.

Q: Would you call yourself a happy person?

I wouldn't have it any other way.

Saturday afternoon in March in Aspen means that the streets are flooded with strollers and shoppers and the shops and galleries are crowded with browsers and lookers. We talked to artist Tom Benton (no kin to Thomas Hart Benton), thirty-eight, in his elegant, severe downtown gallery as the tourists trooped in and out. Our conversation seemed to interest some of them as much as Benton's striking, strong, and completely original prints, posters, and pots. He and his wife and their two children live in an apartment over the gallery. Behind it is a studio and an immense cylindrical kiln. Benton designed and built it all himself. Though he graduated with a degree in architecture from the University of Southern California, he gave it up for painting, lithography, and potting because he didn't want to be dependent on other people's approval of his work.

Compact and intense, Benton is of average height, but he has a very un-average and flourishing beard. He's one of the young bloods who are almost entirely self-sufficient, in the contemporary sense of the word. He talks with passion and humor about the things he cares about, yet he has that calm center that exists in people who are doing precisely what they want to do. He is committed to his family, his work, his life style, and political and environmental decency.

Q: Tell us about your background.
I was born and raised in California. Oakland till I was ten. Then Glendale. Went to Glendale High School and then into the service. After that, I decided to do something with my life. So I went to USC where I got my degree in architecture. While I was still in school, I

worked for some architects. After I graduated, I went on working in architecture. Did several houses on my own. Worked for a firm in Pasadena for three years, doing small commercial buildings. Then I got fed up with architecture, fed up with L.A., fed up with the whole philosophy of living out there.

Q: Why did you choose Aspen?

We first came here in 1958 when I was still in college. We dug it. We were really impressed. There were still a lot of old Victorian houses boarded up and abandoned. Naturally, the skiing was great, but the town was something else! We were like the tourists who come in here now and tell us how much they envy us, living here. We came back again in 1960. It was still a great town with neat people. After I got out of college, we went to Europe and stayed till our money ran out. In college, I had a scholarship and the GI bill and was working twenty hours a week and Betty was working full-time. So we took the money and went to Europe. We've never had more money. When we got back to L.A. I think I was already a little fed up with the place and the people and architecture. So we decided to give it all up, but we had to find a place. There was Big Sur, but something, for us anyway, was missing there. Then we thought of Aspen, so we came out and it was fall and as we drove up the valley, we said, "This is it!" That was 1962. We stayed only one day, bought a lot, went back to L.A. to sell our house and our car to pay for the lot and all the other things we were suddenly committed to. For eight months, I worked like hell—for the highest bidder—to raise money so we could build in Aspen. Funny thing is that through all that time I didn't know what I was going to do here—in the building. I knew it would be on my own, by myself, but I didn't know whether it would be painting, potting, prints, or what. I knew I was going to build a building, but I didn't know what I was going to do with it. In the spring of 1963, I began work on the building. I did nearly all of it myself.

Q: And did you still think that this was it, the place?

No question about it. We suddenly had a whole new life.

Q: How do you feel now?

It's a mixed-up town now. There are a lot of good people and a lot of really bad people. But that's good. It's real. At Snowmass and Vail, they try to make it real, but it's not, it's like a movie set. The heritage of the old mining days makes Aspen unique. It has something you don't find often. The people—most of them—have that same individual spirit that the miners had. Now, of course, we have these bad cats that are more interested in success than they are in that spirit.

Q: Do you think they will succeed in destroying the spirit?

I think they're going to win. I'm a pessimist, but I'm not a pacifist. I think you ought to take your cuts at them. If you're going to go down, go down fighting. Give it a try. It seems to me that it's happening everywhere, so there's no point in running. Lots of people are looking for a new place, but I don't think anyone's found one. You can take the guy out of Aspen, but you can never take Aspen out of the guy. Someplace the battle will be won.

Q: What kind of battle is it?

It's a philosophy battle. There are lots of people here whom I disagree with about lots of things, but they all really love Aspen. But I have no common ground with the exploiters. It's aesthetics versus economics.

Q: How do you fight?

Well, we're always talking aesthetics. Beauty, emotion. It's hard to put into words. It's a feeling. You know when a building or a project works here. They, the exploiters, talk economics only. The two don't meet

anywhere and our side never gets the picture across. Profit interests them, not the long-range view. One problem is that the exploiters are super-organized. Most of us left the structured society. We're free spirits. You can't organize free spirits. But the exploiters automatically stand up for each other. No matter what the issue, they're together. We're not.

(lady in gallery: I couldn't help overhearing. Good luck. Keep up the fight.)

Someday someone's going to win.

Q: Is there another place?

No. Everywhere we've gone, people look to Aspen as a refuge. Aspen is still the place where you can live the way you want to live, do your own thing in a creative way and it's accepted. In fact, it's expected. But it's changing. I see more of the other kind coming in. Every day, tourists say they've been coming here for ten years, but they're not sure about next year. As the town changes, the people who come here will change. When we first came, there was very little promotion. You heard about Aspen by word of mouth, it was an idea. But now, with success, we have to have huge budgets, ads to guarantee great skiing and love. It's a different appeal. It's all economics now.

Q: Are there practical controls?

Not really. The people in control are happy to put people like me on commissions, to let me work, sap my energy, but they still make the decisions. It's a game. They pretend everyone can participate, but only they can make the decisions. We asked that people be allowed to vote on density controls. A simple thing. But they aren't about to allow that. You should be able to work through the government, but you can't. The alternative is what an ecologist from USC called environmental guerillas. Holland has an underground group, the provos. They say, you insist on doing that, we'll blow it up. The

developers say that any restriction on them is in conflict with the American system, but I think the protection of the individual now lies in the protection of the society. That's how the ALF came about.

Q: Tell us about the ALF.

It doesn't exist. No structure. No membership. Just a name. The Aspen Liberation Front. But it's amazing, because we have a name we now get mail from city departments. I could never get those communiques as an individual. But the name makes us legitimate.

Q: Are you going to continue to live downtown?

No. I spend too much time here reacting, so I can't get my own work done. We're looking for land in the country. I'm beginning to sell my work through other galleries, so I don't need to go on selling it myself here.

Q: What are the things you react to?

Well, I'm right in the middle of it here. I see all around me bad planning, stupid solutions to simple problems. It tears me up. The people who do these things have so little sense. Some old-timers have given up. They just want to make it, too.

Q: How much time do you spend on posters?

About a quarter. When I first started doing posters, I did commercial things. Skiers, aspen leaves. Now I do it for myself and they're very popular. If you're really sincere with yourself everything works better. And you feel better about things, too. You just have to do what you feel. When we decided to move here, we sat down and figured it out on paper. That's the way you do things in the city. Well, on paper, it didn't work at all. According to the paper, we should have been on the relief rolls. It never works on paper. You finally begin figuring other ways to figure it. Finally, you throw away the paper and just start. Step by step. The land. The building. The business. Odd jobs. Commercial posters. And then suddenly I was just doing my own thing. And

it worked. We're making it . . . our way. But it would never work on paper.

Q: How do you feel about American people in general?

Most of them are robots. When I go to Los Angeles and I see those people content with smog and congestion and not rebelling, I have to think they've been brainwashed. But the kids make me think it's turning around. Either we're lost or the people are going to make a big change. Everyone in L.A. who's over thirty is set. But great things can happen when these kids reach voting age. Their parents couldn't resist that hard-sell on TV, but maybe they can. Maybe they can avoid opting for the safe life. Lots of kids are afraid to get out of school because they're afraid they'll be swallowed up by middle-class America. All I know is that it's easier for me to make my own decisions than to have someone else make them for me. If someone else decides that you're going to show up for work dressed in such-and-such a way, that's an inconvenience for you. You have to make sure you have the right clothes. If you make your own decision, you just wear whatever shakes out the best in the morning or whatever you feel like wearing. And that seems to me to be easier than having someone else decide for you. It's that simple. And you do a better job in your work, too.

Q: Who are Aspen's young leaders?

Most of them have dropped out. I tried, but I have to fight; I can't stay divorced, I have to take a cut at them. Now I'm categorized as a quack. Someone said I was a recluse. How can you be a recluse in the middle of downtown Aspen? It is ironic that the people who have made the spirit of the place now have no say.

Q: Who's got the power?

Power is money. The great division is the pocketbook. The City Council listens to people with money. So instead of learning from the big cities' mistakes, we emulate them. We're in a footrace to hell.

Q: Is the general affluence of the country having an influence here?

Yes. Definitely. It wasn't here when we came. Now we have jet setters. Strivers. The pecking order is evolving. Art now has a capital A, because of affluence and fads. So if I get in tight with certain groups, I make more money. But the thing is that I didn't come here for that. Like everyone else, I knew what I was getting into. We knew there were off-seasons. Now the new guys want to eliminate the off-seasons.

Q: Is there a simple solution?

Sure. A benevolent dictator. An aesthetic dictator. People want direction and leadership. Anyone who can give that direction, who can line out a philosophy, will get tremendous support. We don't have leaders now. We have a bureaucracy, with a life of its own.

Q: Why did you abandon architecture?

It's a great art. But here, I do what I want to do and then subject it to people and they're free to reject or accept it. In architecture, you have to be a showman. You can't just do it, you have to sell it before you do it. In art, no one really knows. I'm sincere, I'm not perpetrating a fraud, but the judgment of my worth is history's. I don't know if I'm any good, but it's mine and I do it for myself first.

Q: Is your life what you want it to be? Are you happy?

Yeah. I believe you do things according to a kind of inner spirit. Things happen to you at a certain time, the right time. Things always seem to work out. If I wasn't happy, I'd do something else. Life is too short. Why do anything you don't want to do? What would happen if you woke up at sixty-five and began wondering about all the things you didn't do?

But a town is also events. Indeed, any town is as much the product of events as of people. Until 1960, Aspen was unique and beautiful and peaceful, then events conspired to alter the character of the place. Suddenly, Aspen residents found themselves on a roller coaster called success.

Chapter 4 / The Process

A decade ago, the Aspen Post Office was a big room with worn wood floors, flaking paint, hissing radiators, and banks of burnished brass-faced boxes in the first floor of the large, heavy Elks building. Across the street, in an equally venerable building, was the Pitkin County Bank. Almost everyone came once a day to the bank or the post office. They were dusty, mellow institutions in which everyone knew everyone else and the atmosphere was completely casual. In the summer, these buildings were airy and cool, good places to escape the heat of noon. In winter, they offered toasty respite from the snow and cold and they always smelled of wet wool. They were more than merely post office and bank, they were community meeting places. A simple trip to the post office might result in a dinner invitation, an offer of dry firewood, or a coffee klatch, as well as the usual letters and bills. That was 1959, corner of Galena and Hyman, Aspen. Walter Paepcke did not frequent the corner, preferring to divide his time in Aspen between the Hotel Jerome, one of the many local properties he controlled, and his large, serene house on First Street, overlooking Hallam Lake. But his influence was felt there. Like him or not, one had to admit that. He had shepherded Aspen back from hard times as carefully and as artfully as he had built Container Corporation of America from a small, unknown company into an industrial empire.

In April of 1960, Walter Paepcke died. At the time of his death, he was working on plans for a museum of architecture and a four-year college for Aspen, dreams that remain unrealized to this day.

In February of 1961, the gaunt but grand old post office was a food market; the Aspen Post Office had moved into its own ranch-modern building two blocks east on Hyman Street. It was big, efficient, and cold.

In November of 1961, the Pitkin County Bank became the Bank of Aspen, the latest acquisition of the White family of Pueblo, a prominent Colorado banking clan. It was the first major investment of outside money since the arrival of Paepcke. In less than a year, the Bank of Aspen moved its assets and liabilities to an elaborate modern building one block west and one block north, a building complete with a ski-up window and a fireplace and big city ambience. Though the tellers' barred cages had disappeared, an air-cooled impersonality created bars in the mind. The old bank building became a gift shop.

These quiet realignments were hard for many Aspen residents to accept graciously. In less than two years, the man most responsible for Aspen's resurgence had died, their favorite meeting places had vanished, their bank had changed hands and attitudes, and the corner of Galena and Hyman had lost considerable panache. Nothing was quite the same after that. When you throw

a stone into a pond, you cannot stop the ripples.

So it is with a town. When you begin to shuffle the order of things, you are forced—by momentum if nothing else—to keep shuffling.

But things were changing all over the country. John F. Kennedy had replaced Dwight Eisenhower in the White House, for one thing. The American people loved Eisenhower and had he been eligible to run in 1960, he undoubtedly would have won the Presidency again. But, love aside, the country suffered several recessions during the Eisenhower years and a kind of torpor inhabited the people. With Kennedy, new energy and vitality filtered down from the White House into every corner of the land. Everything from new construction to personal income to prices began going up. And unemployment began going down. America was a lively place to be in the early 1960's. Things were happening. More people had more money than ever before. The business community was not overly fond of Kennedy, but it—like everyone else—enjoyed the new wave of prosperity. The word *affluence* became a staple in newscasters' vocabularies.

New life styles were emerging, too. Air travel was becoming increasingly popular. You could go nearly anywhere by plane. It was quick, convenient, and economical. Almost everyone became more mobile. And interest in skiing was growing. It was a sport the entire family could enjoy together. It was exciting. And it was chic.

Both Doc Des Roches of Ski Industries of America, New York, and Steve Knowlton (former Olympic skier, former Aspenite) of Ski Country, U.S.A., Denver, agree that the 1960 Olympics at Squaw Valley, California, transformed skiing from an obscure pastime into a popular sport. Des Roches says that was the turning point for skiing, the year when skiing began to boom. Though

no one in skiing entirely believes any of the statistics, SIA's unofficial figures, gathered by Des Roches, verify the contention that skiing moved from the sidelines into the sporting mainstream in the 1960's. For decades, it had been—like polo or surfing—the sport of rich men or diehards, a vaguely esoteric preoccupation that no one knew much about. In the 60's, it became an essential activity for many Americans. College students, the newly affluent middle class, young families, bachelors, and career girls took to the slopes in ever-increasing numbers. In the winter of 1958-59, 75,000 out-of-state skiers came to Colorado. They spent over $7 million. The following winter, 140,000 out-of-state skiers spent $14 million.

Remote as it was, quirky as it was, Aspen was to feel the impact of America's new affluence and style as much as any town in the country. Growing affluence plus growing mobility plus growing ski fever equals boomtime in ski towns.

The Post Office Department and the banking Whites both saw the boom rolling into Aspen before many of its residents did. After they reacted to the tremors that prefaced what Eric Sevareid called the Aspenquake, other people—principally from California, Texas, Chicago, and Denver—reacted, too, underlining their reactions with cold cash, investing in property in town and in the country around Aspen. When the boom began to rattle local minds, rough, constantly changing battle lines were drawn: locals vs. money men, idealists vs. pragmatists, pioneers vs. dudes.

The locals liked the town the way it was, a natural fortress of light and air and green and good smells. The dudes saw that sweet fortress as a bonanza and set about to mine its riches. The locals were multi-minded and leaderless. The dudes were single-minded and, thus, did not need a leader. Some locals felt that they could

engage in healthy compromise by letting in and, indeed, encouraging the messengers of growth and progress. But you cannot bargain with a flood. Nor can you turn it off when you've had enough.

Besides, growth and progress are basic ingredients of the American Dream. In the late 1940's and 1950's, however, no one thought much about growth and progress in Aspen. Success, to Aspenites, was qualitative, not quantitative. The natives, who had stayed in Aspen through the lean years, simply liked living there. It was beautiful, it was serene, and it was their home. The people who moved there after the war came for a variety of reasons, but none of them had to do with success. Indeed, many of the new citizens had deliberately turned their backs on lucrative futures in big cities. They were mavericks who had concluded at some point that they were not interested in the things most Americans were interested in: comfort, convenience, affluence, big cars, bigger houses. If they had been interested in those things, they would certainly not have come to Aspen where the predominant life style was living gracefully on a shoestring.

Economically, life in Aspen was hard in the 40's and 50's, but, in intangible ways, it was satisfying and serene. For better or worse, neither Walter Paepcke nor anyone else possessed the gifts of prophesy. Neither he nor anyone else expected Aspen to turn into a boom town. The skiing, the concerts, the lectures were all enjoyable and they all lost money for their backers. All enhanced life, but none changed life in the lovely little town. It was Paepcke's intention to complement, not to alter. And so when what William James called "the bitch-goddess Success" shimmied into Aspen in the 1960's, it took everyone by surprise.

In the late 1950's, the locals seemed to have a solid grip on things. In 1955, after an often bitter

struggle, Pitkin County Commissioners adopted zoning regulations for the portion of the county that surrounded Aspen. In 1956, the Aspen City Council passed a comparable code. Unsatisfied with the section having to do with signs, a self-appointed brigade went out on the highway at night and sawed down billboards from Aspen to the county line. It became an after-dinner diversion: men in tweed and flannels would disappear as coffee was being served and return in an hour or two with sawdust on their shoes. Then as now, city residents involved themselves in county affairs and county residents participated, unofficially, in city politics, for everything that happens in the city and the county affects all residents. Finally, after most of the signs had been wrecked, the county acted to phase out billboards. Today, the highway west of Aspen is a remarkably uncluttered road and many residents look back fondly to the years when billboards were the major villain.

II

In 1960, more ominous villains began to emerge. Growth and progress were still dirty words in many Aspen circles. But the city of 1,101 (according to the 1960 U. S. census) adopted the largest budget in its history—nearly $250,000. The city fathers ordered a new water system, hired a city administrator, bought walkie-talkies for the police, and approved a four-story motel for Main Street over the protests of many citizens and the Planning and Zoning Commission. The Chamber of Commerce was not idle either. In the course of 1960, it opened a full-time office with a reservation service, decided to underwrite a national advertising campaign, and discussed hiring an agency to solicit conferences for the town. Not to be outdone, county officials decided to pave more county roads and to widen the lovely, meandering Castle Creek road from eighteen to thirty

feet. Civic leaders were opening wider the door to progress, setting the stage for radical growth.

That year, ski business in Colorado jumped 42%. Reasons for the leap were ascribed to national interest in the winter Olympics, early snows, additional promotion, faster and easier air travel, and expanded facilities around the state. All records were broken in Aspen on February 20 and 21, when 2,500 skiers were counted on Ajax. The miniboom encouraged the sheriff to issue warnings about ski thieves.

Growth was accelerating on other levels, too. The Aspen School of Contemporary Art was founded, the Music Associates of Aspen and the Aspen Institute discussed the possibility of merging, the Aspen Playhouse scheduled several plays, the Aspen Public School doubled its capacity by building a new school, the Smothers Brothers appeared at a local nightclub, the Jerome flew seafood in from Gloucester, an experimental mall on a downtown street was judged a success, a restaurant offered "long thong" specials, and, when a Denver brokerage opened an Aspen branch, it became the smallest town in the country with a direct line to Wall Street.

The Post Office Department considered mail delivery and then decided against it, announcing that their new building would have 900 boxes, as opposed to 460 boxes in the old location. And people wondered who in the world would use that many boxes.

Seventeen students graduated from Aspen High School in 1960.

In some respects, the town seemed to be resisting progress. Overloaded lines caused frequent disruption of telephone service and County Commissioners complained that their chambers were redolent with the smell of horses.

The highlight of the simmering zoning battle in

1960 was a fight, waged by a group the *Aspen Times* dubbed "money-hungry men," to reduce the 200-foot setback on the highway. They lost.

Nimnon, the town's tame elk, was killed in a foolish accident. The Aspen Skiing Corporation raised ski rates for local children from 75 cents to $2, which inspired the Mother's March, a full-blown protest against big, heartless business.

By the end of the year, building permits had reached $3 million and retail sales had topped $5 million. Not bad, some said, for a tiny town in the Rockies. Others were overtaken by gloom.

1960-1961: 1,584,250 skiers in U.S.

1961 was a quietly dramatic year. Building permits and retail sales moved up, but barely. However, the Aspen Skiing Corporation recorded a history-making gross of $650,000 and said that its Christmas business was up 30% from 1960 with an average of 2,400 people using the mountain daily. The Whites bought the bank and the City Council approved another record-breaking budget: $379,471. They also approved deployment of a four-and-one-half-man police force with twenty-four-hour radio service and they issued licenses to twenty-nine motels with 1,135 beds. About midyear, the city administrator quit, citing City Council interference, and was replaced almost immediately.

Various outside entities recognized Aspen's progress in various ways: the state decided to build a new bridge over Castle Creek west of town; the phone company replaced the WAlnut exchange with digits and, over the protests of many residents, built their own building across the street from the Community Church; the post office opened its new building and promptly ran out of boxes; a natural gas company was given the Aspen franchise; the University of Colorado planned to offer extension courses in Aspen; newsman Lowell Thomas

did several news broadcasts from the stage of the Opera House; and *This Week, Newsweek,* and the *New York Herald-Tribune* were among the publications that spotlighted Aspen.

To maintain the town's upward thrust, the Chamber of Commerce advertised in several mass-circulation magazines. But ski thefts were on the rise, too, proving again that every silver lining has a cloud.

1961 was a big year for civic and cultural improvements. The hospital added a $250,000 wing. A nine-hole golf course opened. The Aspen Improvement Association was founded to acknowledge and encourage good architecture. A fund drive was begun to build a new library. The Aspen Institute announced that it would add a physics division. The world's first professional ski race was held in Aspen. School enrollment approached 500. And Alan Drury, Christian Herter, Robert Osborn, Kenneth Rexroth, and Robert F. Kennedy were among Aspen's visitors.

There were sour notes, too. Two dogs were poisoned and several businessmen took the Aspen Music School to court because they objected to the "noise" made by practicing music students in the downtown area.

1961-1962: 1,852,000 skiers in U. S.

Though both retail sales and building permits hovered at about the same level in 1962, it was a momentous kind of year for the town and its residents. And it began with a bang when a Nevada Corporation paid $1 million for an assortment of mining claims and properties and a 1,800-acre ranch up Hunter Creek, northeast of Aspen. Later in the year, the ranch was resold to a Los Angeles developer.

1962 was also the year that the condominium, a variation on the cooperative apartment, came to Aspen, though the state did not pass enabling legislation until 1963. A Denver developer announced plans for a twelve-

unit condominium and sold ten before construction began. Almost simultaneously, a Texas combine announced plans for a condominium complex, with swimming pool, bar, restaurant, and other lavishness at the base of the Little Nell slope. It would cost $200,000. Ski business around the state was up 42% and the Aspen Skiing Corporation announced that its earnings were up more than $40,000. It bought the Aspen Ski School from Friedl Pfeifer to round out its control of Ajax. Moving right along with the growth and progress partisans were the City Council and the Chamber of Commerce. The City authorized a new $175,000 electric system, said it would pave fourteen downtown blocks, imposed restrictions on water use, and passed a whopping $500,000 budget. The Chamber of Commerce collected $12,000 in dues, hired an executive director and a public relations firm, but nixed a snow-making scheme. Other signs of upward movement: $90,000 worth of ski package plans sold, a problem with bus parking and stopping, more poisoned dogs, a record-breaking summer for the Aspen Music Festival with a record number of people, 785, attending the opening concert, and a 30% rise in bank assets in one year.

The media were not unaware of all this activity in the Rockies. ABC-TV planned an hour-and-a-half program on skiing in Aspen, an Aspen film made by Walt Disney was shown on television, the *Saturday Evening Post* did an in-depth and inaccurate piece on Aspen, and CBS-TV devoted an hour to "The Aspen Idea," as it exemplified what they called a Western renaissance. Eric Sevareid lauded Aspen in the *Saturday Review* for trying to preserve what he described as "the spaciousness" of the West.

Civically and culturally, Aspen continued to grow. $100,000 was spent on improving the airport. The National Science Foundation gave $92,000 to found

an Institute of Field Biology in Aspen. Construction began on the $370,000 Paepcke Auditorium, the largest building to be erected in Aspen since the mining boom. The County Commissioners and the City Council voted together to fund a $45,000 master plan for the Aspen area. 634 students were enrolled in the Aspen school. The city fathers gave Canyon Cable TV a franchise for a cable TV system in the area, which would increase the number of channels received from two to six. All by itself in Colorado, Aspen went on Daylight Saving Time. Sevareid, C. P. Snow, Dr. Jonas Salk, Dr. Karl Menninger, David Rockefeller, James Farmer, and Jan DeHartog were among Aspen's summer visitors. Jazzman Dave Brubeck visited his mentor, Aspen composer-in-residence Darius Milhaud. Several people recommended that the city buy up and preserve green space, among them Institute director Robert Craig and architect Fredric Benedict. And, withal, a growing number of letters to the editor reflected a growing concern among the citizenry about Aspen's "image."

Aspen did suffer one downward movement in 1962: it was 40° below on January 10; and one embarrassing moment: someone stole a radio out of the police station.

1962-1963: 2,179,000 skiers in U. S.

But, in 1963, only a few months after he had praised Aspen, Sevareid, by now a regular Aspen visitor, wrote in a nationally syndicated column that Aspen was a "Shangri-la" in danger of being spoiled. Construction topped $4 million and retail sales lept to $7 million in 1963 and, by the end of the year, an increasing number of Aspenites had begun to share Sevareid's concern.

The year began with the inauguration of a brand-new mayor and City Council. The mayor, Harald "Shorty" Pabst, member of the beer dynasty, rancher, Institute and Skiing Corporation director, was the first

non-native to be elected to the post since the mining days. He and the Council, which had run with him on the "Clean Sweep" ticket, immediately cranked up the city machinery. Work began on the new electrical system, a new city administrator was imported from the Midwest, water rates were raised, it was decided that all downtown streets would be paved, and a $552,000 budget was approved. Enrollment in the school rose to nearly 700.

But the municipal activity only echoed increased momentum among the town's businesses. The Texas-based owners of the Aspen Alps Club decided to add a $291,000 sixteen-apartment building to its burgeoning complex. 103 members of the Chamber of Commerce paid over $9,000 in dues and the Aspen Community Promotion Committee, overcome by enthusiasm, suggested that the town erect billboards around the state. The anti-billboard forces, which had successfully rid Pitkin County of the big signs, immediately opposed the idea as cheap and hypocritical. Having decided to install new lifts for the coming season, both Aspen Highlands and the Aspen Skiing Corporation proposed that the town spend $65,000 on promotion, of which they would pay half. Despite generous, free publicity in big mass circulation magazines, it was apparently felt that additional tourist lures were needed.

Added to the roster of amenities were the Brown Ice Palace, an immense indoor rink owned by Mrs. D. R. C. Brown, wife of the Skiing Corporation president, and a radio station, KSNO, owned by *Aspen Times* publisher William R. Dunaway and several others. Additional civilizing influences were the new Aspen Historical Society, the debut of the Aspen Film Conference, the organization of the Aspen Community Theatre, and the first Aspen Jazz Party which brought, through the efforts of a Denver broker and jazz buff,

some of the country's top jazzmen to the Jerome Hotel for a two-day marathon jam session. The first phase of the long-awaited master plan, which would tell Aspenites what to do with their town, was introduced and judged "pretty but inadequate" by the city fathers. The Aspen Institute made national news when it announced that its chairman, Robert O. Anderson, had established the $30,000 Aspen Award, which would be given annually to an outstanding person in the humanities. It also hired Alvin Eurich, a one-time Ford Foundation official, as president. He was the first non-Aspenite to head the AIHS.

Proving themselves stubbornly iconoclastic, a number of anti-organization Aspenites vigorously protested the organization of an Aspen Junior Chamber of Commerce and it sank quickly. Ski patrolmen and lift operators on Aspen Mountain voted forty-three to six to unionize and formed the Aspen Mountain Employees Association, which immediately asked for higher pay and more benefits. A strike was averted at the last minute when the AMEA and the Corporation settled their dispute on the eve of a virtual shutdown of the mountain. On the lighter side, the Smothers Brothers did a one-nighter in Wheeler Opera House.

It was a very good year for businessmen, but more and more people began to wonder if all the success might not be too rich for Aspen's blood.

1963-1964: 2,448,000 skiers in U. S.

The mercury in the success thermometer continued to rise in Aspen in 1964. Building permits rose to $4,770,000 and retail sales jumped to $9 million. The Aspen Skiing Corporation's gross increased by $500,000, businesses and restaurants noted 20% to 40% gains in Christmas business, and the Bank of Aspen announced that its assets had doubled in less than three years. Formed as an extension of the Aspen Community

Promotion Committee, the Aspen Association announced a $70,000 winter promotion budget and a $23,000 summer promotion budget. But the most significant event of 1964 was the U. S. Forest Service's approval of the Janss Investment Company's plans for the $10 million Snowmass-at-Aspen ski area. The Skiing Corporation, which would run the mountain for Janss, opened 10,000 acres to touring skiers. The Corporation also turned down an international race for Ajax, incurring the wrath of the Chamber of Commerce and the Aspen Restaurant Association.

Construction began in 1964 at Ruedi, near Aspen, on the multi-million dollar Arkansas-Fryingpan water diversion project, which Aspenites had bitterly opposed. And the Forest Service decided to pave the Maroon Creek road, which many residents felt would diminish the beauty of that valley. Faced with an ever-increasing enrollment, the Aspen School Board decided to build a high school complex in the Maroon Creek Valley, because land in town was too expensive. The city fathers were busy, too. They decided to build a water collection and treatment plant, to set up an employee clearing center to look into prospective Aspen employees' pasts, to begin a one percent sales tax in 1965, and passed the city's first $600,000-plus budget. Over mayor Pabst's veto, the City Council rezoned a portion of the west end from business to tourist, to keep gas stations out of the area. The giant Humble Oil Company, which wanted to build a station there, promptly sued the city in an attempt to break the zoning code. And one of the aldermen accused the mayor, as an Institute official, and the Institute of supporting Humble in the fight. The Institute denied the charge.

Other significant events of the year were the taking of an option on an immense parcel of land on Owl Creek, one of the approaches to Snowmass, by an Aspen-

Texas combine, a recommendation that density controls be set up in the business and tourist sections which was opposed by the Chamber of Commerce and the Lodging Association, the addition by Aspen Airways of flights to Grand Junction 125 miles west of Aspen, and the phone company's decision to install a microwave transmission system with a hotly contested giant "billboard" on Smuggler Mountain.

Action on the cultural front was less frenzied. Land on Main Street was purchased for the new library, the Aspen Civic Association was founded with the purpose of protecting Aspen through a strong zoning code, and Benjamin Britten, the English composer, was the first Aspen Award winner. The Aspen Music Festival and School moved to its large and serene campus on Castle Creek. The second Aspen Film Conference was held. Pierre Salinger, Alfred Knopf, Walt Rostow, and most of the Kennedy family were among Aspen's visitors. Robert Craig, who had directed the Institute's programs since 1954, resigned. And a new weekly newspaper, the *Aspen Illustrated News,* was founded by a group of people, including Ski Corporation directors, who objected to the *Aspen Times'* editorial policies.

A snowmaker was hired and quickly fired in the most contradictory action of the year. There was no question now: with or without a snowmaker, Aspen's growth was snowballing.

1964-1965: 2,755,000 skiers in U. S.

As if to confirm the phenomenon with physical evidence, the heaviest snowfall ever recorded in Aspen occurred in March, 1965. Also hitting new highs were building permits which reached $5.5 million and retail sales which nearly doubled before stopping at $16 million. There were other equally troubling manifestations of growth: the crime rate was rising; the police closed four delapidated houses and evicted their youthful

residents; an employee registration ordinance, patterned after a Las Vegas statute, was passed; and an 11 PM curfew was imposed on minors. Planning and building went on at an increased pace. While the Planning and Zoning Commission was studying the preliminary master plan (having changed planners in mid-plan) and passing a 37½-foot ceiling on commercial buildings (after an eight-story building was reluctantly approved because it violated no existing regulations), several million dollars were invested in new condominiums and tourist accommodations increased 20%. The *Aspen Times* called parking "a major problem." A Denver corporation bought 2,000 acres of ranch land west of Aspen. The city passed a $700,000 budget, a $3.7 million metro sanitation district was proposed, and the hospital announced a $250,000 addition which would triple the number of beds. Still nervous, some people organized the first Golden Leaves Festival to increase fall off-season traffic.

But with all the boomish atmosphere, the Hotel Jerome was closed for the first time in history; the Institute, which held the lease, tried to sell it, saying they were in the conference, not the hotel, business. Badly in need of repair, the proudest building in Aspen had become a white elephant.

Things were rosier for the ski companies. The Highlands announced that it would build a new lift, the twentieth in the area. As if to celebrate a $600,000 increase in revenues, the Aspen Skiing Corporation announced that all lift rates would go up, including residents'. And the two corporations proposed a $120,000 promotion budget.

National publicity continued, too. The Winterskol parade was televised across the country and *Life* magazine did a sensational and slanted story—for which they staged a raucous party—on "Aspen's Awful Problem—

Surfers on Skis." Though the story was largely fiction, it brought more liquor agents into Aspen. A better kind of publicity was achieved when Humble Oil's lawyers, on arriving for their suit against Aspen, were greeted by a crowd of picketers and credit card burners. Rock Hudson and Robert Wagner came to Aspen to ski, causing a mild ripple of excitement among the tourists.

Perhaps reacting to the increasing number of skiers, novelist Leon Uris, an Aspen resident, and others proposed a private club for the top of Ajax. Citing harassment and over-emphasis on athletics, the school superintendent resigned. A study showed that eleven books an hour were borrowed at Pitkin County Library. The Aspen Writers Workshop was founded. Pioneer choreographer and dancer Martha Graham was given the Aspen Award. 400 people attended the International Design Conference's 1965 sessions and well over 1,000 jammed into the big tent for a Duke Ellington concert, the first time a jazzman ever performed there. The Institute bought *Atlas*, a New York-based magazine which ran selected stories from the international press. The Aspen Center for Contemporary Art was founded. Meadowood, west of Aspen, was the first residential area to use cluster planning to preserve as much open space as possible. Scheduling several seminars to discuss community problems, Citizens for a Better Aspen organized and promised to plump for strong zoning, representative government, city-county cooperation, and better schools. Also seized by community urgency, Woody Creek residents formed the Woody Creek Improvement Association. And, reflecting the general growth, thirty-three students graduated from Aspen High School.

In the winter of 1965, Steamboat Springs, another Colorado ski town, began a promotional campaign keyed to the slogan "There Is No Aspen." By the end of the year, an increasing number of Aspen residents were

themselves encouraging the campaign, tacitly or openly.

1965-1966: 3,101,000 skiers in U. S.

Though skier days were down in 1966, nearly everything else was up. Retail sales and building permits each rose more than $1 million. The Aspen Skiing Corporation spent $500,000 on improvements and planned to spend $50,000 promoting its 20th anniversary. Frozen pipes set a ten-year record. Bank deposits jumped from $2 million to $10 million. A $1.5 million motel was announced. A second business district was planned north of Main Street. The plat for 240-acre Brush Creek Village, west of Aspen, was approved. The $3.5 million metro sanitation district was endorsed by voters. A daily express bus began running between Aspen and Denver. The $180,000 library was opened and newsman Walter Cronkite was the principal speaker at the dedication ceremonies. Snowmass-at-Aspen began selling residential sites. After Robert O. Anderson let his option expire, an 1,800-acre tract up Hunter Creek was sold to McCulloch Properties, a division of the McCulloch Oil Company. The District Attorney called a grand jury to investigate crime and juvenile delinquency and an Aspen chapter of the American Civil Liberties Union was activated to investigate the grand jury and the employee registration ordinance. Local lawyers formed the Pitkin County Bar Association and offered their services to indigent people in trouble. Adam "Batman" West, Defense Secretary Robert McNamara, Senator Charles Percy, and newsman Peter Jennings all skied in Aspen.

A new mayor, another non-native, took office in 1966. He and the City Council passed a $834,000 budget, dedicated the half-million dollar water plant, formed a committee to look into low-cost housing, discussed building a transportation center, rehired Aspen's first city administrator, and faced a mini-crisis when six

of the nine policemen resigned. They also formed a Tourist Department and funded it with $35,000 from the tax on tourist lodging. Shortly thereafter, it merged with the Chamber of Commerce to form the Aspen Chamber and Visitors Bureau. But the Aspen Association, supported in the main by the two ski corporations, was still handling most publicity and promotion. After people objected to the density controls recommended in the master plan, they were cut in half. The Institute sold the Hotel Jerome lease to a group of young Aspen residents.

Three organizations were founded in 1966 to help preserve Aspen and the country around it. They were PARK, a conservation group, the Aspen Valley Improvement Association, an amalgam of large land-holders, and the Roaring Fork Foundation, a land bank. Stan Kenton and his orchestra performed in the tent. The Schweitzer Convocation was held, under the joint sponsorship of the Institute and the Schweitzer Fellowship.

The brightest news of all was that Humble lost in its effort to break Aspen's zoning code. This gave added impetus to the people and organizations which were beginning to agree with the thrust of a badly written and slanted *Nation* article that success was spoiling Aspen and that a major effort must be made to take the slam out of the boom.

1966-1967: 3,496,000 skiers in U. S.

But 1967 in Aspen was a bad year for idealists. For one thing, Freddie Fisher, jazzman, tinkerer, inventor, iconoclast, and free spirit, died on March 28. He epitomized all of the best qualities of Aspen: its free-wheeling style, its independence, its sass, and its idiosyncratic energy. For another thing, in December of 1967, the $10 million Snowmass-at-Aspen ski area and community opened, with a promise that another $65 million would ultimately be spent there. It exemplified

all the qualities which the idealists eschewed: bigness, smooth efficiency, a no-nonsense dollars-and-cents approach, group think, and a victory of pragmatism. Snowmass added 50% more skiing terrain to the Aspen area and, on December 30, over 8,000 skiers were clocked at the four areas with Snowmass topping the list with nearly 2,500. Ski Corporation business was up 46% over the holidays. And why not? There were now twenty-seven lifts in the area. Building permits for the year reached an astonishing $8.2 million and retail sales rose to $18.5 million. 1,700 acres near Snowmass were sold to Eastern developers for $1.25 million. Claiming abuse, the Skiing Corporation eliminated the $1 Aspen area employees' lift ticket and installed a snow-making machine at Little Nell that rattled the entire town. The Corporation also announced that henceforth it would stage and underwrite major ski events. In one of the nicer human touches of the year, Frenchman Andre Roch, who had helped lay out the trails on Aspen's Ajax, returned for the twenty-first running of the Roch Cup.

The city of Aspen was expanding its domain, too. In two separate annexations, on the south and the north, it acquired nearly 500 additional acres and over 600 new citizens. The Hotel Jerome lease had reverted to the Institute and the city began negotiations to take it over as a convention center. The city also acquired a municipal swimming pool and a new zoning code. In a quixotic move, the city fathers entered into what was to be a lengthy battle with their own city attorney. Aspen ski pioneer Friedl Pfeifer accepted the job of executive director of the Aspen Chamber and Visitors Bureau at $1 a year and announced that $40,000 would be spent on promotion and that a computer reservation service would be installed.

1967 also saw several additions to the cultural

agenda, which already seemed overwrought to many residents. The Aspen Center for Environmental Arts and the American Theatre Institute were founded. Former president of Oberlin, William Stevenson succeeded Alvin Eurich in the Institute presidency. India's Ravi Shanker performed in the tent and the *Snowmass Villager,* a weekly supplement, was founded by *Times* publisher Dunaway.

Other indications that the boom was enlarging were a new dog leash ordinance, an application by Vail Airway to begin serving the Aspen area, and an announcement by McCulloch Oil that they would develop their Hunter Creek acreage in the summer of 1969.

And the Vietnam war issue peaked in Aspen when eighty anti-war demonstrators marched to McNamara's rented house on Castle Creek. Another kind of battle began between residents and the Bureau of Reclamation which wanted to build a road up Hunter Creek.

1967-1968: 3,911,000 skiers in U. S.

1968 was a tumultuous year in America and in Aspen. The national bad mood was felt in the pleasure-oriented town. Retail sales lept to $25 million, building permits reached $10.5 million, the city budget topped $1 million, but even the exponents of the boom were restless. Upset by the arrival of hippies in Aspen, a number of businessmen requested that the police "crack down" on them. After several were arrested on charges of vagrancy and harshly treated by the city magistrate, more liberal citizens protested. The area bar association condemned the magistrate's tactics and, when he refused to resign, he was fired. 250 people attended a reorganization meeting of the American Civil Liberties Union. Several hippies took Aspen's police and officials to court in Denver, charging harassment. The *Aspen Times* attacked the anti-hippie elements editorially and a number of advertisers promptly began a boycott of

the paper. To counter the boycott, eighty people signed a four-page ad in the *Times*, supporting its position on civil liberties. Ultimately, the city fathers repealed the vagrancy ordinance.

But councilmen had other problems, too. Because the sewage plant was overloaded, they passed a moratorium on building only to have it thrown out by the courts. Their sales tax was voided after an angry businessman claimed it had been illegally passed. Another protest erupted when an oil company wanted a portion of Main Street rezoned so it could build a gas station near the County Courthouse and St. Mary's Church. The area was not rezoned. The city fathers banned angle parking and set up Aspen's first parking lots, but downtown traffic and parking were still problems. And they accused the Pitkin Iron Company of polluting Castle Creek, one source of city water. Between battles, they discussed low-cost housing, plans for an eighteen-hole golf course, a conference center, and pedestrian malls.

The Post Office Department was having problems in Aspen, too. It finally leased space in a new and controversial $1 million, block-long condominium for its overflow. The phone company introduced direct distance dialing and announced that it would build a $400,000 facility at Snowmass-at-Aspen.

The Janss Investment Company sold its interest in Snowmass to the American Cement Company and Snowmass American picked up its option on an 8,300-acre ranch, thus tripling its land holdings. It also announced that it would add $6 million in new buildings to West Village, opened its Brush Creek Country Club, reactivated the Aspen Film Conference to add some cultural sheen to its agenda, and said that it had already booked eighteen conventions for the summer of 1969.

Things were cheerful for the Skiing Corporation,

too. With a record gross of $3 million and a record 25,906 skiers in one week in March at its three areas, it cancelled all Aspen area employee lift rates, and said it would spend $155,000 on advertising and promotion and another $300,000 on its lifts and trails at Snowmass. It also welcomed Interski, one of the world's most prestigious ski events.

The ACVB said it would spend $122,430 in 1969. Pitkin County Airport, too, was feeling the crunch. Though there were twelve inclement days in March, 2,869 landings were registered. Underscoring all of this, the state tourist bureau announced that one-third of all the skiers who came to Colorado came to Aspen. Not to be left out, the Aspen Highlands announced that a twenty-story, $20 million complex would be built on Maroon Creek, at the base of the slopes. And a seventy-nine-lot subdivision was opened up on Red Mountain. The fate of the Hotel Jerome was finally settled happily, when a man from Michigan bought it and announced his intentions to restore its former glory. The Silver Dawn Mining Company struck silver on the back of Ajax and said the mine could produce $125 million and no one even blinked. Snow, not silver, was the thing now.

On the intellectual-educational front, 800 people attended the design conference, author-critic Edmund Wilson was given the Aspen Award, the Center of the Eye, a photography workshop, was founded, two more "future of Aspen" seminars were held, and the school enrollment passed 1,000, sending the school board into over-time planning sessions and several sections of the first grade into makeshift classrooms in the basement.

By the end of 1968, the size and ferocity of the boom was beginning to frighten more and more people, including some of its earlier advocates.

1968-1969: 4,377,000 skiers in U. S.

But the first months of 1969 indicated that there was no relief in sight. By March, a number of new condominiums were announced (though tourist beds now approached the 12,000 mark) and building permits reached $2.5 million. Sixty-four grand thefts were recorded in two months. Snowmass American sold 8,300 acres that it bought for $2.5 million to a New York-Boston-Aspen group for $5 million. Aspen Airways began Aspen-Las Vegas flights. ACVB dues revenue topped $25,000. Twenty-five million Americans saw Aspen on ABC-TV. The FAA began operating a control tower at the airport. A hippie in California tried to hijack a blimp to take him to Aspen. City and county officials decided to hire a full-time planner. The Ski Corporation announced it would spend $1 million on new lifts and trails at its three areas. A Regional Service Authority—composed of three city councilmen and three county commissioners—was formed to administer receipts of the county sales tax and said that the first $295,000 collected would go to parks and recreation. the airport, the dump, and publicity and promotion. The city administrator showed the Council a $17 million, thirty-year capital improvements budget. The Skiing Corporation bought a lodge to use for employee housing. Two new banks received charters to operate in Aspen. And the Aspen Liberation Front asked the City Council to let the people vote on stiffer density controls and scale controls. The Music Associates of Aspen built new classrooms and practice rooms, anticipating its busiest summer in its twenty-year history. The State Highway Department announced that it had begun planning a four-lane superhighway into Aspen. It would cost about $20 million and of itself attract more cars into Aspen. Militant residents prepared to battle the department.

Bigger . . . more . . . up . . . these are the operative words in Aspen's continuing saga. In the maelstrom,

lines muddy, divisions become arbitrary, idealists turn into pragmatists, and, on occasion, dudes act like pioneers. But affluence has gotten a good grip on Aspen and its citizens. This most unusual town has been dragged, kicking and shouting, into the mainstream, sucked into the system. With fast jets, it is almost as convenient to New York as Bronxville . . . and a lot more interesting. Today it is as easy to get from Los Angeles to Aspen as it is to go from Los Angeles to Palm Springs. In this jet age, every town is a satellite of megalopolis, a colony of the urban areas. Thus, those towns with physical grandeur and emotional charm, with attractive and interesting things to do, with any kind of grace or distinction end up on nearly everybody's map.

1969-1970: 4,900,000 skiers in U.S.

To paraphrase a memorable line from a long-gone soap opera, "Can this remote, little town in the Rockies find happiness as one of America's biggest and most successful resorts?" The answer to the question lies somewhere ahead of us.

As it enters the seventies, Aspen's major dilemma is overdevelopment which is personified by such projects as Snowmass-at-Aspen, one of the new breed of resort towns: planned, computerized, homogeneous, controlled.

Chapter 5 / The Prospect

Twelve years ago, several men stood on the summit of a mountain called Baldy near Aspen. It was wild, high, and remote and they had come there to tame it. Today, Baldy is the mainspring in Snowmass-at-Aspen: Aspen's fourth ski area, a complete community, and one of the most popular new resorts in America.

The chief mover in the taming of Baldy and the carving out of Snowmass-at-Aspen was William Janss of California. A onetime ski racer, flyer, art collector, cattleman, and bigtime Los Angeles land developer, Janss knew what he wanted and presumably got what he wanted, but he and his brother Edwin have now sold their interest in Snowmass-at-Aspen and retreated to Sun Valley, which, according to William Janss, attracts "the power people, the excitement people." While Snowmass was still on the drawing boards, the Janss brothers bought Sun Valley and one can only assume they prefer its ambience to that of Snowmass-at-Aspen. This is not to say that Snowmass does not have its own contingent of "power people." One of its most esteemed home owners, for instance, is Robert McNamara, former Secretary of Defense and now president of the World Bank.

Snowmass-at-Aspen measures thousands of acres. Snowmass American owns much land and leases additional land from the U.S. Forest Service. The ski slopes are wide and immaculate and they range from easy to very difficult. The community, West Village, is pleasant and attractive, arranged for the convenience and comfort of its inhabitants. Upwards of $75 million will ultimately be spent on the mountain and residential and commercial development at Snowmass. The Aspen Skiing Corporation runs the mountain and Snowmass American runs the development. Over $4 million in lots and condominiums were sold there in 1968.

From the beginning, the people in charge have shown some measure of respect for the country they invaded. To preserve as much of the landscape as possible, their master plan clusters people, shops, restaurants, and lodges in villages, rather than letting them sprawl randomly over the meadows at the base of Baldy. This makes economic as well as aesthetic sense; one of the most alluring commodities at Snowmass-at-Aspen is pastoral views. But already the emergence of West Village has permanently and drastically altered the area.

A few miles west of Aspen, two valleys wind off the highway—Owl Creek and Brush Creek. Before Snowmass, they were beautiful and serene ranching areas, possessing a lonesome, lost loveliness, ideal places to escape the twentieth century. The two valleys collide far back in the hills. Just beyond that collision point, West Village rises out of the landscape, all modern, efficient, and radical. It's like coming across a shopping center deep in the folds of the Grand Canyon. Not necessarily evil, but surprising and discouraging. For some reason, West Village looks bigger from the outside than from

the inside. The fringes consist of bulky lodges and condominium apartment complexes. A golf course has been sculpted out of pasture land. Swimming pools shimmer amongst the buildings like outsize jewels. The inner circle consists of shops and restaurants and at the center of it all is a village square—complete with bell tower. Planning and design for the village were done by Aspen architect Fredric Benedict. He utilized much native stone and wood in the West Village buildings. Their design might best be described as simple, tasteful, mountain modern. There is nothing avant garde or way-out about West Village. (Though Benedict wanted to do something truly modern and original in both planning and design, his initial ideas were rejected by the corporate minds which controlled the pursestrings.) West Village is solid, respectable, rich, and comfortable. And it is designed solely for pedestrian traffic. Cars are left at the gates, though there are service roads for delivery and maintenance trucks. One can stroll from shop to shop or sit in the sun to eat a hamburger, somewhat removed from the stench and noise of the automobile. Great gangs of shiny cars are corraled—like cattle—in tiered parking lots at the west edge of the village. Thus, they have been tamed, but not overpowered and are neither out of sight nor out of mind. West Village is a landlocked cruise ship, an enclosure in the wilderness for the affluent, a sedate playground where everything's in its place and there's a place for everything.

Benedict, several west coast designers and planners, and a gaggle of Snowmass American executives are members of the Conceptual Design Group which will oversee future planning, design, and development at Snowmass-at-Aspen. Said Snowmass American president and group member Roland Herberg, "People are our first concern."

The group has recommended an extension of West

Village. A twelve-foot-wide bridge will permit pedestrians to stroll over slopes and lifts from the existing village to the planned appendage to the southeast. Approximately $3 million will be spent on the extension.

Now it is clear that if there were not a demand for land and apartments, Snowmass American would not expand. With $8 million worth of residential properties on the market in March of 1969, the powers-that-are obviously had enough confidence in their product to create more merchandise. It's a simple economic rule: faced with enough demand, you can safely enlarge your supply. In sum, Snowmass-at-Aspen is succeeding.

But what is Snowmass-at-Aspen? It's a ski area with relatively self-contained residential and commercial sections: a ski village, in other words, with its own post office, bars, restaurants, nightclubs, shops, delicatessen, movie theatre, swimming pools, tennis courts, paddle tennis courts, golf course, and miniature golf course. And what do people do there? In winter, they ski, sun, shop, swim, and indulge in the usual variety of apres-ski activities. In the summer, they sun, shop, swim, play tennis, golf, hike . . . but it's not the same without the skiing. In summer, the recreation staff—a variation on the cruise director—must use all of its imagination to keep the visitors busy and happy. In its first summer, Snowmass was not nearly as successful as it had been during its first winter. To fill the gaps, the recreation staff staged a succession of gaudy mini-carnivals— Acapulco Days, Western Days, even a Rocky Mountain Mardi Gras—contrived to pull passing tourists off the road. They also hosted a chess tournament and the reactivated Aspen Film Conference for more advanced minds. Summer 1969 was less frenzied and more profitable. Full-page ads in *Time* and hard personal sell attracted small conventions and conferences, which not only filled lodges, shops, and restaurants with the

expense account set but were also more in keeping with the Snowmass image.

But what is Snowmass-at-Aspen, *really?* It's an instant town, a total resort for "all seasons," as they say in their advertising, that rose up almost overnight in a high country meadow. It has no history, no heritage, no past, no soul. On the other hand, it's efficient, it works, it's comfortable, it's controlled. Snowmass-at-Aspen is a controlled environment. That's the big thing about Snowmass-at-Aspen, that control.

Snowmass American can manipulate the environment as easily as you can manipulate your electric blanket. They can't program the weather. Not yet anyway. But they can and do program everything else: the architecture, the landscape, the mood, the traffic, even the dress and style of Snowmass employees. They maintain absolute architectural control, because—as owners and developers of the area—they can simply refuse to sell land to anyone whose plans are not compatible with their ideas of beauty and harmony. They manipulate the landscape by literally moving trees, streams, and rocks. If, in their view, nature did it wrong, they redo it. That's one of the reasons that many West Village trees are in pots and its streambeds are concrete slots. Water on. Water off. Tree here. Tree there. Flowers today. Bushes tomorrow. Mood control is a subtler business. It's done with lights and signs. Silence! Chess masters at work. Lights up. Happy mood. Lights down. Thoughtful mood. Traffic and people control is the key, however, to everything else. Having carefully worked out the ratio of parking spaces, mountain capacity, restaurants, and shops to tourist beds in advance, Snowmass American can simply turn off the flow of tourists when it reaches its limit and everything else will remain in balance. It's more than a little like *Brave New World,* but it is succeeding.

On big skier days in Aspen, Snowmass ticks off more skiers than any of the other areas. Hundreds of people have bought property there. Thousands have spent time there. Nearly every major magazine has done a laudatory story on Snowmass. It's a hit and that controlled environment is the keystone of its success.

Other places have equally good snow. Other places have equally attractive accommodations and shops. Other places have equally beautiful settings. Other places have everything that Snowmass-at-Aspen has. But other places don't have that control. It took Aspen nearly twenty years to reach a point that Snowmass reached in one year. Anthropologists have always known that, by and large, people like sameness, not difference, that they prefer running with people who are similar to them in status, background, and attitude, that they are uncomfortable with people who are not like them. Snowmass American has turned that anthropological rule into gold.

The men who are in charge at Snowmass-at-Aspen are very much like the vacationers who visit there. Solid, respectable, conservative, careful, straight out of Middle America. They are efficient, paying attention, nice people and they run a nice place for other nice people. This is not to say that they would discriminate against anyone, bar him from staying there. It is to say that the manipulated niceness of Snowmass-at-Aspen itself excludes some people. It's not *their* kind of place and they know it before they get there. Thus, the solid, respectable, careful atmosphere is seldom sullied by weirdos, freaks, crazies.

Aspen, which has a love-hate relationship with Snowmass-at-Aspen is not a controlled environment. It has a turbulent history, a complex heritage, and a sometimes overpowering soul. As Snowmass may be the ultimate in one-dimensional, homogeneous communities, Aspen is probably the ultimate in multi-layered, heter-

ogeneous towns. Rich and poor, square and kook, middle class families, students, artists, working men—every variety of human being can be found in Aspen. And often they run head-on into each other. Clash. Bang. Zap. Seldom an actual banging of heads, often a real difference of minds.

So here they are: the instant, homogeneous, planned, controlled community and the rich, diverse, heterogeneous, quirky free community sharing the same valley, the same landscape, the same natural resources in a kind of geographical and sociological high noon. One is lavish in history, buffeted by time and fate, built with sweat and dreams, growing spontaneously. The other has no history, is unscarred by time and fate, built with slide-rules and computers, growing according to a firm corporate design.

Snowmass and its counterparts across the country are a signal from the future. They exemplify the new breed of small town, made—like some intricate tool— to do a specific thing, to fill a specific need. Places where urbanites go to escape the less pleasant aspects of city life. Products of the technological age. Towns without pasts, substance, or roots. Rootless towns for the new breed of rootless men. Playgrounds for harried city dwellers. Enclosures which protect their inhabitants from the realities of life. It's nice, but is is life?

There are people who think that Aspen and Snowmass-at-Aspen can make it together, can go on prospering, civic arms linked. In fact, they are like oil and water, day and night. The very success of the controlled environment bruises the spirit of the freewheeling, contradictory place that is Aspen.

For better or worse, Snowmass's influence on Aspen is large and permanent. The American Cement Company is making a major investment in Snowmass and it will therefore use all of its considerable corporate clout to

succeed on a scale larger than most Aspen residents can even imagine. To make its ever-enlarging development possible and profitable, Snowmass will need an ever-escalating number of customers. Whether or not Aspen wants that kind of quantitative success, it has arrived. And with it have come all of the problems of success. But because Aspen has many masters and Snowmass has only one, the problems strike harder and with more force in Aspen than in Snowmass-at-Aspen. It is a perfect example of the tail swinging the tiger. Aspen, the tiger, is at the mercy of Snowmass, its tail. Indeed, the development of Snowmass has already changed the character of the Roaring Fork Valley. There is a momentum, a kind of fever, which reaches all the way from Aspen to Glenwood Springs. Many new developments are in the works. A major installation, the multi-million-dollar Aspen Wildcat, will be constructed very near Snowmass by a group of Boston and New York investors. Brush Creek Village, Holland Hills, and other mini-cities are being planned. A Houston-Aspen group holds an immense parcel of land on Owl Creek. There is talk of "industrial parks" near the airport and there is new activity in Basalt and Carbondale.

It is impossible to say, of course, that all of this action wouldn't be taking place without Snowmass-at-Aspen's emergence as a major resort. Perhaps the triple explosion of money, people, and leisure time nationally spelled the end of tranquility in the Roaring Fork Valley anyway. But it does seem fair and reasonable to say that Snowmass has been a major factor in the new, sometimes frantic movement in this no longer remote section of the Rockies.

Chapter 6 / A Postscript

Affluence has a dark side which threatens unique places and unique people. America's future is full of Snowmasses-at-Aspen. As the good old towns die or are absorbed or changed, new controlled environments will replace them. But will they really replace them? Will they offer the sense of history, of identity, that America's small towns could offer their residents? Or will they be simply plush, look-alike way stations in a country where nearly everyone is utterly mobile?

In our rush toward uniformity, in our effort to standardize everything from education to production, from life styles to death styles, perhaps there is no longer room for quirky, complex small towns. Perhaps—like the flivver and the butter churn—they have outlived their usefulness. Perhaps—like the bald eagle—they are fatally out of synch in this jet age where everyplace is as close as your airport and almost everyplace looks like everyplace else.

And what we don't or can't tame or standardize, we foul. Americans seem to have a genius for befouling their environment. We have allowed billboards, auto graveyards, and neon explosions to separate motorists from the country they are traveling through. We have allowed factories to pour their wastes into our rivers and pump their noxious, filthy fumes into our air. We have allowed strip mines to destroy thousands of acres, tearing up the countryside and leaving an ever-enlarging wasteland in their wake. We have allowed lumbermen to chew up our forests. The list of permitted assaults on our environment is endless and it is dismal proof that our belief in a man's right to make a buck is stronger than either our respect for our environment or our love of nature. As long as the dollar rules the American roost, only a fool would be optimistic about the environmental future of America. Many people have devised ways to stem this insane destruction of our cities, small towns, and countryside, to bring things back into balance; but none of the theories—however radical and imaginative—will work, for it is the materialistic, anthropocentric nature of the American people that is leading us over the edge and down into environmental chaos.

From the beginning, the majority of Americans have consistently allowed economics to be put above aesthetics. Only now are we beginning to reap the grim harvest of that crass attitude and to realize that the highest standard of living in the world has been the direct cause of the spoliation of much of our countryside and the disintegration of our cities. We did not mean to poison our water and our air, scar our hillsides and valleys, destroy the balance of nature, and turn our cities into concrete nightmares. But everything indicates that we are too far down the road to doomsday to turn back.

There is little hope for restoration in the cities. They are worn out and, in many cases, bankrupt.

Nothing much can be done about the dying towns—until or unless urbanites migrate to them, seeking relief from urban miasmas. Nothing much can be done either about the towns which have been absorbed by megalopolis. They are in the whale's belly and they will stay there, beyond redemption.

But we can save the good small towns like Aspen—for a while anyway. They are our most valuable man-made resource. River towns, ocean towns, plains towns, mountain towns—we need them all. They are America at its best and most basic and they are very good places to live. More than ever before, we need their neighborliness, their virtue, their stability, their relative immunity to the flash and phoniness of modern life. There is no such thing as the Garden of Eden and there never has been. Paradise, if it exists at all, exists more in one's head than in fact. Every place has its ragged parts; no small town is free from flaw. Indeed, some small towns are narrow and vicious prisons where anyone straying from the norm is vilified and occasionally ostracized. But, by and large, the good small towns in America give their residents more than they take away from them.

We must therefore resist the trend toward homogenization, the mania for turning every place into a replica of every other place—each with its complement of Chicken Delights, A&W rootbeer stands, Holiday Inns, and Texaco stations. We must defend the good small towns as stoutly and stubbornly as the Sierra Club defends the redwoods and Grand Canyon, for they are our only socio-geographical entities that have not run away with themselves. The good small towns—Aspen; Concord, New Hampshire; Woodstock, Vermont; Steamboat Springs, Colorado; Camden, Maine; Bodago Bay, California; Sedona, Arizona; Salmon, Idaho; and hundreds more—must battle the efforts of tourists and developers to turn them into look-alike towns where comfort and convenience are kings and efficiency and ease matter more than evergreens and evensong. If, for a while, we can preserve these gentle oases, they will give us—all of us—much more than clean air and water and a human scale. They will give us solace, serenity, hope, and a sense of humanity.

Stringent zoning codes, imaginative planning, ecological inventories, conservation and preservation laws at the Federal level (akin to their conservation of wilderness areas), and a determined effort on the part of residents of the good towns to resist the temptations of easy money will delay the arrival of ruination. It is too late to hope for more.

Appendix

Photographers

FERENC BERKO settled in Aspen in 1949 at the invitation of the late Walter P. Paepcke. Born in Nagyvard, Hungary in 1916, Berko became seriously interested in photography when he was 12. He studied philosophy at the University of London while also working as a still documentary photographer and movie producer-director-cameraman. When he was 22 he traveled to India where he worked 10 years making industrial and commercial films. In the summer of 1947, Berko came to America at the invitation of the late Moholy-Nagy to teach at the Institute of Design in Chicago. Berko has had photographs published in most of the major publications and all the major photo magazines in the U.S.A. and Europe. Some of his prints are in the permanent collection of the Museum of Modern Art. Since moving to Aspen, Berko has traveled extensively in Europe, Japan, Thailand, Greece, Turkey, and Mexico.

ROBERT CHAMBERLAIN, 32, a free lance photographer and film maker, came to Aspen in 1959. Born in Kansas City, Chamberlain studied philosophy at the University of Colorado and did graduate work in mathematics and Oriental philosophy at the University of California, Berkeley, and the University of Hawaii. His work has been published in *Majority of One*, *The San Francisco Oracle*, *Aspen Magazine*, and national ski magazines. Chamberlain has created numerous posters, has worked on several short films and has exhibited his photographs in both Aspen and San Francisco.

DAVID HISER, a long time resident of Seattle, graduated from the University of Washington with a BA in English. An expert climber, Hiser spent three years after college exploring the high country of the west. He came to Aspen in the fall of 1964 and became chief photographer of the *Aspen Illustrated News*. Now a free lance photographer, Hiser, 32, has had his photographs published in several national magazines including *The National Geographic*. Hiser's wife, Cheri, also a photographer, is director of Aspen's photographic workshop, Center of the Eye.

JOHN M. SMITH worked for newspapers in the Aspen area before becoming a staff writer and Picture Page Editor for *The Louisville Times*. He also was a reporter and photographer for the *Middletown* (N.Y.) *Times-Herald Record*. He now teaches reporting and photojournalism at University of California, Los Angeles.

OTHERS: Bob Brougham of Aspen. Gene Voss. Staff photographers of the *Aspen Illustrated News* and *The Aspen Times*. Unknown and unnamed photographers whose record of early Aspen is part of the permanent collection of the Aspen Historical Society.

Captions

DEDICATION. Hiser

CHAPTER I

page 3   Mili Street, looking north, with Wheeler Opera House. Chamberlain.

page 5   Victorian house on Francis Street. Chamberlain.

page 7   Lifetime Aspen residents. Berko.

page 9   Aspen rancher. Smith.

CHAPTER II

page 15   Winter morning, Galena and Hyman Streets. Smith.

page 17   Winterskol parade. Berko.

page 19   Oldtimer. Berko.

page 21   Glidden house, Hallam Street. Berko.

page 23   Hotel Jerome, New Year's Eve. Smith.

page 25   Skier. *Aspen Times.*

page 27   Hikers, Maroon Bells. *Aspen Times.*

page 29   Court House statue. Berko.

page 31   Main Street, west end. Chamberlain.

page 33   Racer on Ajax. Chamberlain.

page 35   Aspen from Red Mountain. Berko.

page 37   Early Aspen. Aspen Historical Society.

page 39   Load of silver ore. Aspen Historical Society.

page 41   Ticket. Aspen Historical Society.

page 41   On Hallam Lake. Aspen Historical Society.

page 43   Early parade. Aspen Historical Society.

page 45   Early Aspen resident. Aspen Historical Society.

page 47   Aspen panorama, 1890's. Aspen Historical Society.

page 49   Lucas Foss, Izler Solomon, Amphitheatre. Berko.

page 51   Aspen Health Center. Berko.

page 53   Institute guests. Berko.

page 55   Sculptor Irv Burkee. Smith.

page 57   Climber. Smith.

page 59   Aspen Raceways, Woody Creek. Chamberlain.

page 61   Rock dancer. *Aspen Illustrated News.*

page 63   Thinker. Chamberlain.

page 65   West end. Berko.

page 67   Easter race. Voss.

CHAPTER III

page 73   On Cooper Street. Chamberlain.

page 74   Aspen gardener. Berko.

page 75   Restaurateur. Smith.

page 76   Bookshop. Smith.

page 77   In a mountain cabin. Chamberlain.

page 78   Race day on Ajax. Chamberlain.

page 79   Winner. Chamberlain.

pages 83, 85, 87   William Noonan. Chamberlain and Smith.

pages 91, 93, 95   Fredric Benedict. Smith and Chamberlain.

pages 103, 105, 107   Katie Lee. Chamberlain and Hiser.

pages 113, 115, 117   Wayne Vagneur. Smith.

pages 133, 135   Tom Benton. Smith.

pages 137   Benton with former Secretary of Defense Robert McNamara at peace march. Hiser.

CHAPTER IV

page 145   Gingerbread. Berko.

page 147   Liquor store. Chamberlain.

page 149   Aspen encounter. Chamberlain.

page 151   Morning walk. Smith.

page 153   Cabin. Chamberlain.

page 155   Condominium. Smith.

page 157   Highway. *Aspen Illustrated News.*

page 159   Bus stop. Smith.

page 161   Colorado Governor John Love, Paepcke Park. Smith.

Captions Continued

page 163   Aspen Amphitheatre. Hiser.

page 165   Children's parade. *Aspen Illustrated News.*

page 167   Aspen protest. Brougham.

page 169   *Moving. Aspen Illustrated News.*

page 171   Condominium. Smith.

page 173   Bedroom. Smith.

page 175   Sleeper. Chamberlain.

page 177   Football game. *Aspen Illustrated News.*

page 179   ACLU meeting. Chamberlain.

page 181   Night 1. Smith.

page 183   Night 2. *Aspen Times.*

page 185   Saint Mary's Church and Rectory. Smith.

page 187   Church and trucks. Smith.

page 189   Trampoline, west Aspen. Smith.

page 190   Swimming pool. Smith.

CHAPTER V

page 197   West Village, Snowmass. Hiser.

page 199   Snowmass tower. Smith.

page 201   On Snowmass square. Smith.

page 203   Sleigh. Smith.

page 205   Skier. Smith.

page 207   Condominium. Smith.

page 209   Landscape. Smith.

Cover. Smith

Authors' photos, Smith, Edward P. McDonald, Jr.

Jacket design, Clifford and Smith

Acknowledgements

We would like to acknowledge the help that the Aspen Historical Society, Pitkin County Library, the *Aspen Times*, the *Aspen Illustrated News*, *Times* editor William R. Dunaway, and lifetime Aspen residents Judge and Mrs. William Shaw gave us in this enterprise. The Society and the two newspapers generously opened their picture files to us. In addition, the *Times* gave us free access to their back issue files. Mr. Dunaway, the Shaws, and a number of other Aspen residents read the text and gave us valuable and pertinent advice. Without their help our task would have been considerably more difficult. We would also like to thank Aspen—not only for being, but for being such a special and unique place. Without it there would have been no book at all.

PC and JMS